THE PATH BACK HOME
Real Stories from Siletz, Oregon

Copyright © 2011 Good Catch Publishing, Beaverton, OR.

All rights reserved. Written permission must be secured from the publisher to use or reproduce any part of this book, except for brief quotations in critical reviews or articles.

This book was written for the express purpose of conveying the love and mercy of Jesus Christ. The statements in this book are substantially true; however, names and minor details have been changed to protect people and situations from accusation or incrimination.

All Scripture quotations, unless otherwise noted, are taken from the New International Version Copyright 1973, 1987, 1984 by International Bible Society.

Published in Beaverton, Oregon, by Good Catch Publishing.
www.goodcatchpublishing.com
V1.1

Printed in the United States of America

Table of Contents

	Dedication	9
	Acknowledgements	11
	Introduction	15
1	A Father's Pursuit	17
2	Secrets of the Wind	41
3	Warrior Heart	73
4	Hand On My Heart	93
5	Love Story	109
6	Available	143
7	Accepted	175
	Conclusion	189

DEDICATION

We dedicate this book to all those whose lives are in
situations and circumstances that seem to be
overwhelming and who feel like they have no hope.
As you read, it is our anticipation that you will find there
is a source of second chances that eagerly desires
to welcome you home with unconditional love.

ACKNOWLEDGEMENTS

I would like to thank Vance and Kate Lindstrom for their vision for this book and for the hard work, prayer and faith they put into it to make it a reality. And to the people of Siletz, thank you for your boldness and vulnerability in letting us "see" you in this compilation of real-life stories.

This book would not have been published without the amazing efforts of our project manager and editor, Peter Bell. His untiring resolve pushed this project forward and turned it into a stunning victory. Thank you for your great fortitude and diligence. Deep thanks to our incredible Editor in Chief, Michelle Cuthrell, and Executive Editor, Nicole Phinney Lowell, for all the amazing work they do. I would also like to thank our invaluable proofreader, Melody Davis, for the focus and energy she has put into perfecting our words.

Lastly, I want to extend our gratitude to the creative and very talented Ann Clayton, who designed the beautiful cover for *The Path Back Home: Real Stories from Siletz, Oregon.*

Daren Lindley
President and CEO
Good Catch Publishing

The book you are about to read
is a compilation of authentic life stories.
The facts are true, and the events are real.
These storytellers have dealt with crisis, tragedy, abuse
and neglect and have shared their most private moments,
mess-ups and hang-ups in order for others to learn and
grow from them. In order to protect the identities of those
involved in their pasts, the names and details of some
storytellers have been withheld or changed.

INTRODUCTION

Hope isn't enough. What we all need is a hope that is based on reality. We desperately need the hope that comes from knowing that someone else has "gone through the fire" of life and not only survived, but has found a life worth living.

This book is filled with stories like that.

They are all real-life experiences of people you might know. As you read this book, you will recognize the depth of challenging circumstances that many people have endured. They may even sound remarkably similar to your own experiences. The stories of hope in this book have not been modified or dramatized, nor exaggerated or inflated. They are stories of real people who either made less than ideal choices or were victims of painful (and sometimes savage) circumstances that caused some of life's greatest difficulties. Their stories are wrenching, yet 100 percent true. In some cases, names have been changed to protect related parties from embarrassment by being unnecessarily exposed.

The fascinating part is how these broken people were able to make decisions that resulted in authentic life change. The individuals to whom these things happened are not perfect people. They don't ride off into the sunset, never to encounter difficulty again. Rather, like everyone else, their past is like a haunting shadow that can still exert

THE PATH BACK HOME

its influence in unguarded moments. Yet, in the midst of that, they have learned to overcome and press on by choosing to change their focus.

These real-life stories come from people I'm privileged to know personally, people who are like family to me. We offer them, hoping to inspire and encourage you in your own journey down life's path.

Your friend and fellow struggler,
Vance Lindstrom

A FATHER'S PURSUIT
The Story of Cameron Brown
Written by Karen Koczwara

It was the phone call every parent dreads.

"Is this Cameron Brown?" came a somber voice.

"Yes," I replied slowly, my heart skipping a beat. It was the Fourth of July, a fun-filled day of patriotic festivities. My teenage daughter had headed out with some friends a few hours ago, promising to be back before dark.

"There's lots of drunk drivers out there!" I called out as she walked out the door. "Be careful!"

"I'm always careful, Dad," she replied with a smile and a playful roll of the eyes.

But I still worried, as any father of a teenager would.

"This is the hospital. Your daughter's been in a serious car accident," the somber voice continued. "She's alive but injured."

"Accident?" I grew weak as I gripped the phone with both hands. *Alive but injured.* She was alive! "I'll be there as soon as I can," I said, trying to catch my breath as I hung up. My head pounded along with my heart as I frantically searched for the car keys. My fingers shook so badly the keys rattled, clinking together like chimes as I raced for the car. The nearest hospital was 20 minutes away. It would be the longest 20 minutes of my life.

When a life is at stake, suddenly nothing else matters. The cheery red, white and blue décor that marked this

THE PATH BACK HOME

previously festive, fun day was now a blur along the road, hardly important now. Had I told my daughter I loved her when she sauntered out that door? Oh, how I hoped I had.

I shouldn't have let her go. Her friend was an inexperienced driver, having just gotten her license a few months before. She'd piled a bunch of kids into a Jeep; everyone knew how dangerous those things were. The unanswered questions plagued me as I pressed my foot to the accelerator, those 20 miles feeling like 60 as I sped up the road.

Please, let her be okay. Please. My mind flashed back a few decades to my own parents' nightmare. Their 5-year-old son, fighting for his life in a hospital bed; an accident that shook them to their core. Now I knew how they felt. Now I had a taste of their anguish, an inkling of the uncertainty that lies in the unknown.

Let her be okay ... let her be okay!

☙☙☙

I was born in 1966, the era of the Beatles, the Beach Boys and fast muscle cars. Like most young boys, I enjoyed a good adventure. Growing up in a little Northern California town, I found no shortage of trees to climb or outdoor fun to enjoy. My father was a lineman and worked hard to provide for our family; my mother waitressed and drove a school bus to bring in extra money. My sister, Shelly, two years my senior, kept busy making sure I stayed out of trouble — which, most days, I did.

A FATHER'S PURSUIT

We lived in the mother lode gold country, where remnants of mining days from a century before made for great fun. My friends and I explored old mining shafts, splashed in the public pool on hot summer days and tromped through the nearby swimming holes at the river, where we enjoyed a good mud fight or two.

One day, when I was 5 years old, I climbed up a tree to retrieve my beloved football. As I reached the last branch and stepped out precariously to grab it, my foot gave way, and I plummeted 30 feet to the ground. The next thing I knew, I was waking up in the hospital, my terrified parents hovering over my bed.

"Oh, Cameron! You're awake!" My mother leaned in, her eyes dark with concern. "Do you remember what happened?"

I shook my head, confused. *Where was I, and who were all these guys in uniform bustling around me?* My head hurt, I knew that much. "Where am I?" I stammered, rubbing my eyes.

"You're in the hospital, son," my father replied, patting my head. "You fell from that tree right onto your head. Doctors said your injuries were within a quarter inch of your spinal cord. We thought we were going to ... lose you." His voice trailed off, and he gazed at me as though meeting me for the first time. "We're so, so glad you're okay."

I didn't know much about the spinal cord, but I figured it must be a pretty important body part if everyone seemed so concerned about it.

THE PATH BACK HOME

"Can I go home now?" I asked, still confused.

"Not yet, son. The doctors need to keep running tests. Don't you remember anything? You were knocked out pretty hard," he said quietly.

"Not really. What was I doing in the tree?" I asked.

My parents exchanged glances. "Getting your football down, I believe. The football made it to the ground, and so did you ... on your head," my father explained. "Guess someone was watching over you."

"Like angels?" I asked, eyes wide. I'd heard grownups say this before, that someone was watching over them. I didn't know much about angels, except that they often topped trees at Christmastime and looked pretty nice with their gold halos and clean white robes.

"Could have been," my mother agreed with a smile. "We were so worried we might lose you that we had the priest come over and baptize you last night," she added. "You know, just to be sure."

"To be sure of what?" Now I was more confused than ever. And my head was really starting to hurt.

"Well, you know, to be sure you would ... we'll talk about it another time. Let's see if we can get you some Jell-O. Does that sound good?" My mother tried to change the subject as she waved down a nurse.

I tried to remember climbing up that tree to get my football. My brain felt fuzzy, like when I drank too much soda pop or stayed up way too late on a Saturday night. Well, as my parents said, I was going to be okay now, and that was all that mattered.

A FATHER'S PURSUIT

I spent the next week in the hospital while doctors ran tests, poked at me and gave me lots of bowls of Jell-O. They used big words I didn't understand, but my mother translated their language to me, explaining that I'd sustained a head injury but was going to be just fine. Good as new, even. I was anxious to get out and get back to playing outside, but I decided to stay away from tall trees for a while.

I had godparents who attended the local Catholic church and took me with them for special classes sometimes. My teacher stood next to a picture of Jesus hanging on a cross and helped us memorize Bible verses. Sometimes she read stories to us, like Jonah and the Whale and Noah's Ark. I liked the stories well enough, but they seemed more like a fantasy movie than history. I tried my best to soak up everything, reciting the verses over and over until my brain hurt. I figured it was the least I could do for God, since he saved me from death when I fell out of that tree.

"Do you believe in God?" I asked my father one day.

He shrugged. "I don't know, son. I believe in some sort of greater power, but I'm not really sure what it is."

Curious, I asked my mother her thoughts on God. "Oh, sure. I believe in God," she said quickly. But she didn't say much after that.

In the fifth grade, I started trying to figure out what made people "cool." It seemed that all "cool" guys got into fistfights. One day, I spotted a pretty girl and made a comment about her to another boy.

THE PATH BACK HOME

"That's my girl. You back off, you hear?" he retorted.

On impulse, I took a swing at him. He looked pretty harmless, but before I could regroup, he jabbed me in the face with his fist. I tried to come back, but he hit me several more times, finally knocking me on the ground. I slowly stood to my feet; stars danced in my eyes, and I was dizzy and bruised. I had learned my lesson about trying to pick fights.

Though I stopped climbing trees, I found trouble of a new kind instead. One weekend during a Boy Scout camping trip, one of the older scouts pulled us into his tent. "Look what I got," he whispered, sliding a glass bottle out of his backpack. "You guys ever tried whiskey?"

I shook my head, my eyes widening as I stared at the bottle. I'd smelled it once on an old man at a party, and it was so strong it nearly took my breath away. "Where did you get that stuff?" I whispered back.

He grinned. "I've got my ways. Or should I say, my dad's got a pretty well-stocked liquor cabinet. He'll never notice this thing is gone." He unscrewed the cap and took a long swig, swallowing bravely before passing it to me.

"I dunno." I held the bottle in my hands like a loaded gun; did I dare try it? "Is it gonna make us drunk?" I asked.

He rolled his eyes. "If we drink enough of it. Isn't that the point?"

I wasn't sure I wanted to be drunk. I'd seen drunk people falling down and making fools of themselves on TV; it didn't look all that fun. But then, I didn't want to

A FATHER'S PURSUIT

miss out, either. If these guys, older and cooler than me, thought drinking was fun, maybe I should give it a try. Slowly, I tilted my head back and took a long swig as I'd seen my friend do. The stuff was so strong I shuddered, my eyes watering as I began to choke. "Whew! That stuff's crazy!" I blurted.

"You just had a sip! You gotta have more than that!" My friend grabbed the bottle back from me and drank some more. "Bet you never thought Boy Scout camp could be this fun, huh?" He laughed.

Later that night, when I stepped out of the tent under the stars, my head began to throb, and I felt dizzy and weak at the knees. If this was what being drunk felt like, I wasn't sure I liked it. All I wanted now was a good nap.

Back home, my friends introduced me to other types of alcohol and pot, too. I didn't love the stuff, but it seemed to be what all the "cool kids" did. Maybe, if I started young, I'd find my way into the popular crowd by the time I reached junior high.

But when I was 12 years old, my father announced we were moving to Oregon. "It's beautiful up there. You'll love it. More trees in one square mile than in all of California," he added with a laugh.

I was on the cusp of adolescence; it was a less than ideal time to pick up and move. But my father said the work opportunities were better up there, and I saw his point. I'd just have to find my way into the cool crowd in Oregon. And I was pretty sure I knew how to do that.

Within days of moving to our new little town, I'd

THE PATH BACK HOME

found a new group of friends who did drugs and drank. Desperate to be popular, I hung out with them, smoking weed behind buildings after school and downing booze on the weekends. One day, a guy approached me after class. "Dude, why do you hang out with those guys?" he asked, motioning toward the tables where my friends sat.

"What do you mean? They're my friends," I replied defensively.

"Yeah, but, dude, smoking weed and drinking, that's for losers. You don't want to be messin' around with that. Everyone knows stoners are the ones who end up working the fast-food drive-thrus for the rest of their lives."

"Really? Well, yeah, that won't be me. I'm going to college," I retorted. But as the guy walked away, I thought long and hard about his words. I glanced over at my friends, their bloodshot eyes hidden beneath dark hoodies as they laughed at the tables. Maybe he was right; maybe I didn't want to hang out with these guys after all. Maybe there was another "cool" crowd I could join, a crowd that wasn't headed for a career flipping burgers and making minimum wage.

To prove my strong work ethic, I looked for "piece work," where the amount of money one made depended on how hard one worked. In the eighth grade, I took up sheep shearing at a local ranch. I got paid a dollar for each sheep I sheared, but it was tough on my body, so I decided not to pursue it as a career. It tapered off over time. I tried picking brush next, harvesting evergreen boughs from the forest. The money was decent, but the hours were terrible,

A FATHER'S PURSUIT

and I had to work outdoors rain or shine. I decided I'd keep up my grades in high school so I didn't end up doing hard labor or working drive-thrus as an adult.

During junior high, my mother started attending a local church. "You should try out the youth group," she suggested. "Seems like a pretty nice bunch of kids." My parents, though always loving and supportive, had never encouraged me to go to church much growing up. But now that I was just a few years from becoming a man, I'd begun thinking hard about my future. Though I played basketball, got decent grades and had plenty of friends, a certain emptiness had found its way into my heart. I didn't know where it came from, but I was anxious to find a way to fill it. Maybe a new group of church friends would be just the thing.

I liked the youth group well enough. The songs were pretty cool, the games were fun and the people seemed down to earth. The youth pastor got up at the end of the meetings to give a short message. "This week, remember that no matter what you do or where you go, God is with you. He will never leave your side. If you're needing help with a test or feeling stressed about stuff going on at home, you can talk to him about anything."

I thought about the Catholic classes I'd attended as a kid. Though I'd memorized lots of Bible verses, I'd never much understood the point. To my father, God was an uncertainty; to my mother, he was real but not too exciting; and to me, he was some guy up in the sky taking notes, much like Santa Claus does when he writes out his

THE PATH BACK HOME

"good and bad" list every Christmas. This was the first time I'd heard someone talk about God like he was our friend, and I liked it. Maybe I'd try talking to God on my own.

Though I kept attending youth group, I still experimented with drinking on occasion. *I'm not addicted; I'm just having a little fun,* I told myself. I vowed to never get hooked on drugs, as I didn't want to mess with my basketball game. I kept up my grades, which made my teachers and parents happy; from the outside, I was doing just fine.

One of my favorite classes was shop. My teacher was a great man, always positive no matter how crazy his day got. When I asked him his secret, he didn't hesitate to share. "I'm a Christian," he said cheerfully. "It's God who gets me through the day. Do you know God, Cameron?" he added, looking me straight in the eye.

"Oh, sure," I replied vaguely. "I know him." But in my heart, I knew I didn't know him the way this guy did. Something was different; it was written all over his face.

"One of the most important things in life is integrity," he went on. "As you get older, you'll have lots of temptation come your way. The secret is to stand up for what's right and not sacrifice your good judgment just to get somewhere you want to go. Doing the right thing will always pay off."

I nodded as I cleaned up my stuff before the bell rang. I'd never heard anyone speak so candidly; my parents were great people, but didn't have much to say when it

A FATHER'S PURSUIT

came to morals and staying on the right track. I realized I'd been a bit of a wanderer the past few years, like a Boy Scout lost in the woods without his compass. Partying was fun, but it wasn't getting me anywhere. With high school graduation just around the corner, I had even more serious things to consider.

After high school, I set off for Southern Oregon State College, a place where the campus was just as pretty as the girls. There I found another whole set of temptations waiting. "You only get to live once, and college is it!" my peers reminded me when Friday night rolled around.

Though I was confident of my career direction in engineering, the rest of my life felt uncertain and blurry. I found a college church group that met Monday nights and decided to give it a try. I liked it okay, but I was still enticed by the partying world, the one where I mistakenly believed the good life awaited me.

"What's your name?" A pretty girl sauntered up to me at a party one night.

I'd had a few beers, giving me just that boost of confidence I needed to make the next move. We chatted a while, and within a few hours, I gave in to my desires. The beer, women and partying began to blur together after a few weekends. My youth group days and the words of my wise shop teacher became a fading memory.

"How many of you grew up believing in a God you could not see and were told to have faith?" my philosophy professor asked one day. "Pretty far-fetched if you think about it, right? We've got science, and it's proven stuff.

THE PATH BACK HOME

We've got history documented, and it's proven stuff. But believing in a God you cannot see? That's just for fools."

I shifted uncomfortably in my seat as he spoke. I'd been warned about this at youth group, about the "liberal" views many college professors held. But the more educated I became, the more doubts I began to have. Maybe my professor was right. Maybe all those Bible stories I'd heard as a kid, like Jonah and the Whale and Noah's Ark, were just a bunch of fancy fairytales. After all, a guy surviving three days in the belly of a whale without being chewed into pieces? That did seem pretty farfetched the more I thought about it.

But a God that may or may not exist wasn't the only thing on my mind. I met a beautiful, slender brunette, Anna, a couple years into college, and we soon fell in love. A grad student at Oregon State, Anna was easygoing, fun, smart and charming, all qualities of someone I wanted to marry. We dated for two years and then married in September 1990. I was thrilled to have found my soul mate, but something deep down still gnawed at my heart.

A year after we married, I graduated college and landed my first engineering job in Eastern Washington State. From there, we moved to Iowa for work, where Anna gave birth to our first child, a daughter we named Shantell, in 1994. The next few years were a whirlwind of diapers and sleepless nights as our second child, a son we called Tacoma, came along, followed by his brother Jostan. We made our home in a little rural town just outside Des Moines and fell into a happy routine as a family of five.

A FATHER'S PURSUIT

But the long drives back to Oregon to visit family grew taxing, along with the cold Iowa winter nights and endless muggy summers.

"I'd love to get back to Oregon for good," my wife told me. "What do you think?"

"Someday, for sure," I agreed. As I stared out the window at the thick blanket of snow that had piled up on our driveway, I couldn't help but sigh. We had a good life ... a nice house on a generous piece of property, three great kids and a decent income. But something was still missing. "You ever get the feeling we're supposed to be doing something more?" I said quietly.

My wife smiled. "What do you mean? Like taking up bungee jumping or something?"

I laughed. "No, just ... you know. Maybe going to church or something." I hadn't set foot in church in a few years, and I'd begun to miss it. Anna hadn't been raised in church and didn't talk much about God. She believed having a Master's degree and a positive attitude were the tickets to a successful life, and I had tended to agree. Until now.

I dunno. It seems our life is pretty fulfilling the way it is, I thought to myself. *No need to complicate things, right?*

Right, I guess. As the snow started to fall again, the chill inside me grew. I had to believe there was more.

As the children got older and life got busier, the emptiness in my heart grew, and I turned to food for comfort. When I had a bad day, I reached for a plate of

THE PATH BACK HOME

cookies, Jo Jo potatoes with ranch dressing or steaming nachos and devoured the whole thing in one sitting. I didn't think much of it at first, but I soon realized how much food consumed my life. I thought about what I'd eat the moment I woke up and dreamed about it as I climbed into bed; I even ate when I wasn't hungry.

Outside the kitchen, other problems brewed in our house. I'd always been prone to a short temper, but nowadays, I flew off the handle at the children and my wife when things didn't go my way.

"Kids, get in here, and pick up this mess! Now!" I screamed, my eyes fiery as my children sheepishly filed into the living room.

"Sorry, Dad," they mumbled, picking up their things and trudging out of the room.

"Don't let it happen again!" I hollered down the hall. *Where did that come from?* I wondered. *Why did I just get so angry?*

A week later, I took things out on Anna. "How could you forget to pay that bill?!" I screamed at her. "Aren't you thinking straight?"

Anna shrank back, hanging her head. "Geez, Cameron, you don't have to get so irate," she replied hotly.

What was the matter with me? I didn't mean to hurt the ones I loved, but it seemed lately everything made me angry. I tried to get control of myself, but before I knew it, I was yelling again.

I'd always prided myself on being a good, loving father and a faithful husband, but these days, everything from

A FATHER'S PURSUIT

money to a messy house to sassy kids set me off. My great life was beginning to feel not so great.

One day at work, an attractive woman stepped in to speak with me. "Do you have a moment?" she asked, smiling to reveal perfectly straight white teeth.

I tried not to stare at her long, shapely legs as she took a seat across from me, but her beauty was distracting. "Sit … sit down," I stammered. "How can I help you?"

As we spoke, I grew flustered. My mind wandered to places it hadn't gone to since my college days, and I found myself wishing her skirt was just a bit shorter. When she stood to leave, I stared after her, dirty thoughts flooding my brain. I twirled my wedding band and tried to replace the thoughts with those of my beautiful wife, but it didn't work very well. I thought about the woman the rest of the day, half wishing she'd saunter back in the room for another chat.

These lustful thoughts continued over the next couple years. Nearly every woman I came into contact with, from the sales clerk to the coffee barista to my wife's friend, became a sexual object. I became distracted as they spoke to me, trying not to stare at their chests and think bad things. Though I still had eyes for my wife, they now wandered so frequently that I nearly felt I'd cheated on her. The more I tried not to lust, the more I lusted, much like a child who tries not to crave sugar while walking through a candy store.

But women weren't the only thing I lusted over. I decided that whatever I wanted, I would get. One day, I

THE PATH BACK HOME

sauntered into a store to buy a newspaper. As I went to pay, I noticed a magazine I'd been eyeing for some time. I discreetly slipped it between the newspaper as I approached the cashier. As I headed out the door, I prided myself on being so sly. It was just a magazine, I reasoned. I wasn't really hurting anyone. Besides, I was overall a good person. I didn't do drugs, I wasn't divorced and I hadn't cheated on my wife. Life could be much worse.

But sometimes, my conscience tugged at me. "What's wrong with me, God?" I whispered into the air one morning as I got ready for work. My wife slept peacefully on the bed, her dark pretty curls swirled around her face. I loved my wife, my kids and my life. From the outside, we looked like we had a pretty good handle on things. But my secret struggles behind closed doors — gluttony, pride and lust — were eating away at me. I knew God must not be too happy with the person I'd become, but it had been so long since we'd set foot in church, I wondered if he even listened to me anymore.

In 2000, a job opportunity arose in Oregon, and we moved back to the place we called home. We settled into our new house, where my wife raised goats on our property. The kids were growing older, and suddenly I realized I was becoming the very father I didn't want to be. My own father had given me little spiritual direction growing up, never quite sure what he believed when it came to God and the Bible. He'd left me to figure out the world for myself; my high school shop teacher was the only strong moral role model I'd ever had. I'd spent long

A FATHER'S PURSUIT

enough dabbling with the world and all it had to offer. It was time to return to church.

"I'm ready to take the kids to church," I announced to my wife one day. "We're back in Oregon; it's a fresh start for all of us. I think it will be really good for them to be exposed to church, you know, to give them a moral base."

My wife raised a skeptical brow. "Okay, I am willing to give it a try," she said with a sigh.

We knew of a little church called Siletz Gospel Tabernacle just down the road. We had children the same age as the pastor's children, and we knew he and his wife pastored that church. We liked them as people, and we decided we'd check it out one Sunday morning. I dusted off my old Bible, piled the family into the car and headed off to church.

The minute we walked in the doors, we were greeted by warm, friendly faces. As I sat through the service, I realized how good it felt, how familiar, even after all these years. I thought about my church days as a child, youth group as a teen and then college group as an adult. Though I'd often strayed, I always returned, because deep in my heart, I'd always known I belonged. I was done "trying on" the world. I was ready to come home, back to my roots, back to the only one who could help make things right in my life.

"So glad you came this morning!" a few folks called out and waved after the service.

"We'll be back," I assured them.

That evening, I discussed the church service with my

THE PATH BACK HOME

wife. I knew she hadn't had much exposure to church over the years and had her doubts. "I am still a little skeptical about this whole church thing, but I'm willing to go back," she said reluctantly. I felt skeptical, too, but I had a deep spiritual sense that we should somehow be there.

"What about you guys? How did you like it?" I asked the kids next.

They nodded. "It was good!" they replied.

A certain peace warmed my heart, more comforting than anything I'd felt in years. I knew God and I had a lot to work out, but going back to church was a start. We had finally come home.

☙☙☙

"Thanks so much for coming!" Sarah, our new friend, flew across the room to say hello to my wife. "It was so nice of you to make it to my 16th birthday party."

"Of course." My wife gave her a hug. "Thanks for inviting me!"

Though young enough to be her daughter, Sarah had become a good friend to my wife since we began attending Siletz Gospel Tabernacle. Sarah loved God with all her heart and shared his love with my wife by encouraging her in her newfound relationship with God. It had taken Anna a few months to warm up to the idea of God and church, but as she saw the genuine love around her, she sought it out for herself. After she accepted the Lord into her life, my wife's skepticism grew into a heartfelt desire for God. I

A FATHER'S PURSUIT

loved seeing her turning that desire around as she encouraged others. God was doing a good work in her.

After giving my heart back to the Lord, I prayed about the secret struggles that had controlled me for so long. I had prided myself for years on being a "pretty decent" person, reasoning that I'd never done anything terribly wrong. But the gluttony, pride and lust that had worked their way into my heart had subtly distracted me from enjoying a truly freeing relationship with God. Slowly, the morals I'd once held had slipped away one by one as I dabbled with these things. Perhaps certain sins weren't really so bad after all, I'd reasoned.

Though I never hit rock bottom, spinning out of control, I finally realized that I could not truly enjoy freedom in Christ while enjoying the things of the world. I wanted to be free to serve God, love my wife more wholly and be more dedicated to my children. I knew I could not do these things without first breaking free of my chains.

"Lord, I need your help. I can't stop lusting over other women. Please take this desire away from me," I prayed one night on my knees.

To my amazement, the very next day, the sexual desires I'd struggled with since my youth completely disappeared. Though several attractive women came into my path that day, I didn't feel an inkling of lust toward them. "Wow, Lord, this is amazing!" I cried. "You completely took it away!" Even as I'd prayed, I'd wondered if God could really do something as drastic as this, but his power had proven greater than my addiction. I was so

THE PATH BACK HOME

encouraged, knowing that I now had a new power in him.

I hope he didn't take the desire completely away, I thought to myself.

One look at my wife told me he hadn't. I was attracted to her, perhaps more than ever, and in a very special way. God had blessed us.

As I pored over my Bible one night, I stumbled across a wonderful verse, 2 Peter 1:3-4: "His divine power has given us everything we need for a godly life through our knowledge of him who called us by his own glory and goodness. Through these he has given us his very great and precious promises, so that through them you may participate in the divine nature, having escaped the corruption in the world caused by evil desires."

I re-read it several times, my heart rejoicing over the powerful words. God's divine power had given me *everything* I needed for a godly life. I did not have to succumb to the burdens of my past. I could simply call on him and ask for help, for in him I would find strength. What an amazing comfort.

While anger and pride had once controlled my heart, I now took a new approach to my valued relationships in life. My wife and I attended a seminar to help us communicate better; the leader reminded us that in loving each other, we were showing love for our heavenly father as well. God restored my relationship with my wife, catapulting our marriage from good to great. I hoped my kids would see the way I respected my wife as they grew older.

A FATHER'S PURSUIT

"Dad, we're gonna be late!" my son called out one evening, waiting impatiently by the front door.

"Coming!" I grabbed the car keys, and we set off for church. I was so thankful to call Siletz Gospel Tabernacle our home. Pastor Vance and his wife were so genuine, much like the rest of the people we'd met. We'd seen many prayers answered, including our own, since first attending. God was truly working there, and I was so thankful that my kids had gotten involved in the wonderful youth group. The leaders deeply cared for each kid and tried to help them transition from teens to adults, transferring the knowledge they'd gained in church to real life. And though my children were no longer little, I'd begun working in the children's ministry. It was exciting to see young children grow physically, socially and spiritually before my eyes. I wanted to help them build a good foundation that could carry them for the rest of their lives.

As we sped down the road, the sun setting over the Oregon landscape, I realized something profound. Many of my struggles were the result of not being equipped to transfer my knowledge of God as a child to my adult life. The Bible stories about Noah and all his friends had been nice, but they hadn't penetrated my heart; I did not see *why* or *how* they applied to my daily life. But now, in my mid-40s, I recognized just how applicable and exciting the Bible was. My relationship with God no longer sat on the back burner; it remained up front and center. The more I learned about him, the more I wanted to spend time with

THE PATH BACK HOME

him. I did not expect my struggles to disappear, but I now knew I could experience victory through Christ.

This past Fourth of July, my faith was put to the test when my daughter's friend rolled her Jeep, catapulting three of the four passengers out of the car. My daughter was buckled in the passenger seat and somehow remained in the vehicle. It was every father's worst nightmare, making that long drive to the hospital, praying I'd find my baby girl okay. But God was watching over my daughter that day; her only injury was a serious case of road rash when her arm hit the gravel. My heart lurched when I saw her lying there, bandaged and bruised but very much alive. In fact, none of the four of them died — even though three were thrust from the car.

"This could have been the worst day of my life," I whispered, my eyes filling with tears as I hugged her fiercely. "Don't do that to me again, promise?"

"Promise," she replied, grinning despite her pain.

I thought of my parents' own terror years ago when I lay unconscious on that hospital bed, their hearts pounding as they waited for me to wake up.

It took a scare of my own to realize just how crazy a parent's love is for his child. It also reminded me just how much God loved me, the child he called his own, his beloved. Like a loving father, he'd waited patiently for me as I drifted in and out of church, dabbling with the things of the world, unsure if I wanted to completely surrender to him. When I finally did surrender, he didn't chide me for going astray but instead wrapped me lovingly in his arms,

A FATHER'S PURSUIT

just as I'd done with my daughter. And from that moment on, my life had never been the same. I'd found victory, freedom and life in Christ.

And *that* was the secret to the good life.

SECRETS OF THE WIND
The Story of Terri
Written by Christee Wise

My spirit plunged as the small plane made its descent into the little civilization cuddled in the cove. Clouds had pressed heavily upon us the entire flight. The wooded cliffs, the sky and the icy blue-gray sea closed in around me. A heavy weight crushed me. The commuter plane splashed unceremoniously on the earth and slithered down the muddy runway in a village that I imagined had barely altered since pioneer days.

Hoonah had no theater or bowling alley and no paved roads. More worrisome, the town had no hospital and only two weather-permitting ways in and out, by air or by sea. In fact, the remote settlement seemed to clutch the very edge of the earth. The weathered houses of Hoonah grasped the face of forested mountains sloping to the shoreline. Boats and fishing vessels clung to the fringe of ocean, and it jostled them carelessly. I couldn't tell what held the Southeast Alaskan town together with the rain washing down and the tide washing up.

I had always been strong, independent and smart. Raised in Montana, the only girl sandwiched perfectly between two brothers, I was not afraid of living in Alaska. But at 24, uncertainty threatened to break the white-knuckled grip I had on a life spinning out of control. Reaching within myself, sheer desperation prompted this

THE PATH BACK HOME

last ditch effort to find a solid anchor to hold me in the relentless winds and waves of disappointment, hardship and isolation.

Moving to Alaska was the idea of my husband, Jason. He'd come to look for work six months prior. Once he found a steady job and once our baby had finally spent as much time outside of the hospital in Spokane, Washington, as he had struggling to survive inside its Neonatal Intensive Care Unit, Jason sent for us.

Climbing out of the airplane, I held 10-month-old Casey to my chest and wondered if what held Hoonah together was strong enough to hold our family together. Rumors had been trickling back to Kalispell that Jason was cheating on me. I spotted Jason sauntering casually toward us from the airport, and a lump of doubt gathered in my throat.

I swallowed hard and forced a smile. "Hi. Here we are."

"Hi!" He grinned broadly and reached to take Casey and kiss me at the same time. Rugged and good-looking, filled with excitement at seeing us after so many months, his greeting taunted my aching heart. Experience reminded me I dare not trust.

I tried to prolong the embrace, shaken by the strange surroundings and ambiguity of the moment. Was this a new beginning or the beginning of the end for us?

Over the next days, I met his friends and co-workers. Each new face and personality brought to mind one we'd left behind. Jason simply had a head start on me.

SECRETS OF THE WIND

Obviously, he'd already locked in with drug pins here as he had in the Lower 48. Had he given up the drinking and the drugs, I'd have been optimistic about a fresh start for us. Since he had not, my hope crumbled.

Bewildered, I subconsciously determined to take it one day at a time. *He's Casey's dad,* I thought. *Besides, I've been no angel.* Habits I'd given up during pregnancy I welcomed back as my comforters after our son was born 15 weeks premature.

ಞಞಞ

For what should have been the last trimester of my pregnancy, I had commuted between home in Kalispell, Montana, and Spokane, Washington. I spent a few days at a time with Casey in the hospital in Spokane, staying with friends of my parents.

Days after I was released from the hospital, Jason and I bumped into old friends in Spokane. In their company, we numbed our tattered nerves with late-night binging. I came to depend on this routine.

I had to return to work in Kalispell, since my job was our only source of medical insurance. Jason continued to falter in near-unemployment, taking odd jobs and trying to keep his son Ben in school in Kalispell.

When Jason left for Alaska, my younger brother moved in to help me with expenses. He, too, liked to party, and our house became Party Central.

ಞಞಞ

THE PATH BACK HOME

Casey was born at 10:03 p.m. on May 1, 1986 at Deaconess Medical Center in Spokane. He weighed 1 pound, 11 ounces and was 13½ inches long.

"Please, please!" I begged each one on the medical team in the delivery room to tell me what was happening. They coordinated life-saving procedures with solemn murmurs.

"Can I see him? Is he going to be all right?"

"She didn't deliver the placenta. Prep for D and C," I heard the obstetrician order.

"The anesthesiologist is standing by," his assistant answered quietly.

"My baby?"

"Ma'am, they're busy working to stabilize him." The obstetric nurse in pink scrubs tried to reassure me. She spoke gently through her matching pink mask and touched my hand. "You need to relax. Let us take care of you."

I lay back and moaned weakly as the anesthesia began to pull me away into unconsciousness, away from the horrible nightmare.

Jason paced nervously. Dozens of doctors and nurses busied themselves between me and my tiny newborn baby in the next unit. My mother was the only other family member there.

Professionals had decided to life-flight me from Kalispell to Spokane. After three ultrasounds, doctors could not delay labor and delivery. My hometown medical team presented grim odds.

SECRETS OF THE WIND

"Your baby will have a 5 percent chance of survival if you go to the neonatal unit in Spokane. I'm afraid that's better than we can do here," my doctor stated matter-of-factly.

Mom tried her best to encourage me. "Honey, you're going to be okay."

"But what about the baby?" I cried.

Hours after Casey was born, I woke in the strange hospital in a mental fog. I had never even heard of premature birth and thought hopefully it was just a bad dream. My hands lay on the mound of flannel sheets they'd piled on top of me. Panic overcame me. Tears of frustration and fear spilled onto the pillow.

"We're going to move you to Recovery," a different nurse told me, her cheerfulness bizarre proof this nightmare was real.

"Take me to see my baby," I insisted.

She leveled a professional gaze on me, yet her eyes flickered with compassion. Through the swinging double doors, I saw a conference of green surgical scrubs and white coats into which she inserted herself.

An eternity later, she pushed back into the room with a NICU nurse. I caught a whisper, "The mother ... only opportunity ... baby alive."

"The baby is very, very small. He just wasn't ready to be born," the NICU nurse explained. "We're going to wheel you in to see him, but you need to be prepared."

Rolling into the NICU, I peered past the staff and into the immense incubator. A knife went through my heart.

THE PATH BACK HOME

Casey hardly looked like a human baby at all. His body was covered with dark hair, but his skin revealed an intricate tangle of blood vessels under its transparent surface. Outside, he was wrapped in a tangle of wires and tubes. Still, I absorbed as a mother does, every detail of my newborn.

Inches away, he seemed a thousand miles from my reach. Laying on my side, I pressed my hand against the plexi-glass. "I love you, Casey."

No one could explain why my baby had arrived so far ahead of schedule. Working, not feeling well and a shaky marriage were all stressors. But my own anesthetized conscience accused and condemned me.

The dope, the booze, the promiscuity, even an abortion — of course, this is my punishment.

Casey doesn't deserve this, I began to reason with God. He'd never held my attention before. *Please don't let him suffer for what I have done.*

I bargained with God continually as we kept vigil. "I will do anything, *anything*, God, if you will just let my baby live and be okay."

ಊಊಊ

I could hardly feel his tiny body inside of the blanket. He'd gained back the weight he'd lost at first but still weighed only 1 pound and 11 ounces. Casey had survived one month.

"We are going to take him off the respirator," our son's

SECRETS OF THE WIND

pediatrician said that morning. "We're optimistic. You may take him out and hold him."

I held him for less than 60 seconds. In that time, I tried to will into my son the strength to live.

Almost as soon as I nestled him in my arm, a nurse's voice sounded from far away. "It's time. We need to get him back in the Isolette."

Casey struggled to breathe on his own. Alarms beeped and buzzed continually, and my nerves jumped at each sound. I could not stay that day.

Often we'd arrive at the NICU and see an empty bed that held a baby the day before. The truth was too terrible to speak. Someone's child had died.

Most of the babies were bigger than Casey. *If they didn't make it, what chance does Casey have?* The disabling thought began an unbearable cycle of anxiety and guilt. Every day, as I approached the unit, terror would rise in my throat that Casey would be gone.

A few days after we held Casey for the first time, Jason took his son Ben back to his mother in Idaho and headed for Alaska with a friend. He took the $1,500 we'd scraped together. Friends in Kalispell held an auction and placed containers by cash registers in stores around town to raise money to help us. My husband left me alone and broke in the biggest storm of our lives.

Abandonment and rejection rushed in with gale force.

How could you? I screamed inwardly.

☙☙☙

THE PATH BACK HOME

"Mommy and Daddy are going out tonight," Mama explained as she pushed another spoonful of applesauce into Dougie's mouth.

Dougie still needed to be fed, but I was old enough to feed myself. I looked over at Donny shoveling macaroni and cheese into his already filled mouth. He was nearly 6.

"Where?" he asked with his mouth full.

"Bowling league," she replied. "Jerry will watch you. You'll be good, won't you?"

"Sure," Donny said. I stopped chewing and nodded my head. Something felt funny in my tummy, and my feet stopped swinging under my chair.

I swallowed and stirred my mac-n-cheese around on my plate. I imagined Jerry would want to read me a story. It was nice that he paid attention to me. But it felt strange when he'd set me on his lap. His hands were very big, and he liked to feel under my clothes.

"Then the big bad wolf said, 'I'll huff and I'll puff, and I'll blow your house down,'" Jerry read. I wanted to run away like the three little pigs and find a safe brick house in which to hide.

Jerry's voice changed as he shifted me up and down in his lap, and I'd get confused about the story. He made me touch him and touched me in ways no one else had ever touched me. It didn't hurt, but I felt odd and uncomfortable. I wanted to ask Mama about it, but I didn't know how and thought I might get in trouble.

Jerry molested me repeatedly during the time I was 3, 4 and 5 years old. He was the first but not the last predator

SECRETS OF THE WIND

to target me. Older male cousins easily intimidated me, and my confusion grew as their groping and touching vaguely disturbed me. Relationships I formed with men were like stick or straw houses that left me defenseless within a pretense of safety.

☙☙☙

I stared at my shiny black church shoes sticking out in front of me. My legs were almost long enough to let my feet swing under the wooden pew. Donny could do it. Mother held Douglas in her lap, and Daddy held the hymnal so she could sing the words of the songs or read the liturgy. We came to church every Sunday.

In elementary school, I was a straight-A student. The expectations in Sunday school and confirmation classes weren't any more difficult to meet.

"The Apostle's Creed," the pastor began. As though someone pushed a button on a recording, I recited in monotone with the rest of the congregation.

My eyes and mind surveyed the crowd. I counted the number of people who had been to our house to play cards or had gone camping with us. My parents had a lot of friends and enjoyed socializing. Every card game and campout included a fair amount of drinking.

Still reciting, I wondered if Dad had noticed that his *Playboy* collection was disturbed. I knew it was wrong when I found them, but I was curious. I wondered if my brothers had sneaked a peek, as well.

THE PATH BACK HOME

I wondered if I'd be like the women in the centerfolds. The images got stuck in my head.

The recitation was over, and I blinked to bring myself back to the present. During the sermon, I wondered, *What does any of this have to do with anything?*

I started drinking and stopped going to church when I was a young teenager. Our parents made us go until we were confirmed. After that, my brothers and I all dropped out.

ৰ্চৰ্চৰ্চ

Eric started the car. "So, what's going on with you two, huh?"

An internal heat wave swept through my face. I didn't like Eric much, but I didn't have my license or a car yet, and I needed a ride home from the party. To make matters worse, my ex-boyfriend, Kevin, sat in back.

"Well, you guys have been dating for a long time, right?" Eric dredged for information. "So how far did you go? Did you let him feel you up? What?"

I wanted to die, to throw the door open and jump.

Why doesn't Kevin stop him? I thought. But he didn't, and Eric kept going.

Eric droned on relentlessly. His questions became more pointed and personal. "Why wouldn't you sleep with Kevin? He's a great guy. Ya' know that's what he wants."

"Pull over," I demanded. "Let me out!"

Before the wheels crunched the gravel shoulder, I

SECRETS OF THE WIND

yanked the door open and flung myself into the night. Had it not been for my rage, I would have collapsed with grief. Instead, I stumbled two miles to my house in the dark, letting the tears flow. Nothing relieved the ache of realization that other girls had given Kevin what he wanted. I had not, and I'd lost him.

As malformed as my attitude was about sex, I had always believed you should get married if you wanted to have sex.

Men are jerks! They only want one thing. Well, they aren't going to get it from me, I swore. *Screw them!*

Determined not to be used, I yielded to a fury of rebellion blasting up from inside. Throughout high school, I used alcohol. I used every drug I could get a hold of, and I used boyfriends; but I never let anyone use *me*.

By the time I graduated, I had little direction beyond having a good time. I joined a group called Young Adult Conservation Corp to get out of Kalispell. YACC moved us to Idaho, fed us, housed us, worked us during the days and let us party all night.

To house a mob of unruly teens, YACC had acquired a former mental hospital, McKelley Hall, as a dormitory. We were convinced that the spirits of the tormented patients still haunted the hallways.

"I swear I heard footsteps last night," someone began as we clustered outside on the grass, passing joints or draining bottles of whatever someone bought with a fake ID.

"... and crying," someone else would add. "It scared

THE PATH BACK HOME

the s*** out of me. Started down at the end of the hall … it got louder and louder until it stopped by my door." They trailed off and someone else picked up the story.

"That's bulls***," one of the guys said, laughing. "You're just trippin'. Man, you can't handle the pure stuff we got this time."

My roommate nudged me, and we guffawed uncomfortably. Secretly, we were relieved to have another real person with us at night. Making light of our fear was all we could do to quell the fear of our own miserable ghosts.

One night, I was alone and suddenly awakened. A dark presence, blacker than anything I'd ever seen in my life, entered the room. Wide-eyed in the darkness, I distinguished the outline of a faceless being standing between me and the door I knew I'd locked. I lay frozen, too terrified to scream as the Black Thing came closer and loomed larger.

Suddenly, I felt myself trapped by what felt like heavy plastic sheeting rising up from the mattress. It slid up and around me, holding my arms and legs tightly to my body. The Black Thing had no arms or hands, but as it bent over me, the zipper of the body bag closed slowly and securely around me. Beginning at my feet, the zipping crawled past my knees and waist. Reaching my chest, which no longer rose or fell with breath, the zipper stopped abruptly. The being then kissed me on the heart and forehead before closing the bag completely. As quickly as it had come, the being was evidently satisfied, and it left me.

SECRETS OF THE WIND

Springing from my bed, I hurled myself out the door. Light from the hallway spilled into the room. I looked to the left and saw nothing. I looked to the right. Again, I saw nothing but dull tile and deteriorating plaster.

The meaning of this apparition troubled me. Something evil was claiming me. In the light of day, I forced it to the back of my mind. Yet, unable to tolerate my helplessness, I spent most of that year stoned and drunk.

At 18, I returned to Montana. Because I had no purpose, I found myself tossed around on whims and passing pleasures. Even the determination to remain a virgin had gone.

"I'll marry you," Ryan told me. We'd been living together for five or six months, almost as long as we'd even known each other. My suspicion that I was pregnant had just been confirmed.

"I want to take responsibility for you and the baby," Ryan proclaimed with obvious heartfelt sincerity.

Though I'd been willing to shack up with him, I had no desire to get married or have his child.

"I'm not ready for either one," I declared and decided to have an abortion.

I went to the clinic alone.

Convincing myself it was my only option, I accepted mild revulsion as a good teacher and put the ugly event behind me. *I won't let that happen again.*

The relationship soured. As if my soul had been removed, I moved dispassionately from one boyfriend to

THE PATH BACK HOME

the next, one straw house at a time, until I landed in Thompson Falls, Montana, living with Tom.

Jay's Bar-n-Grill was full. I kept busy serving meals and drinks to the crowd of locals getting off work. Around 10 p.m., the crowd began to thin, and I noticed one customer watching me.

I'd never met Jason, but I knew of him. In this little town, most business was everybody's business. Jason's business was that his wife was fooling around.

"I'm Jason. Can I buy you a drink?" He was 10 years older than me, but attractive and charismatic. He'd kept a group of logging buddies laughing all night.

"Sure. I'm off at midnight," I said.

We spent the night drinking, talking and carrying on. That week, I left Tom. Jason left his wife, and we moved in together.

Jason was very charming, but he was already beyond recreational drug and alcohol use. He had become dependent in several ways. Unfortunately, his logging business folded, as well as a couple other business ventures. Selling drugs became easier than looking for work.

We moved to Myrtle Creek, Oregon, to live with his aunt.

"Pincushions!" I locked accusing eyes on Jason. "All they're doin' is shootin' up all the time."

Jason's dark look in return was a warning. "What's it to you?"

Normally outspoken, I didn't have an answer. I felt

SECRETS OF THE WIND

trapped. Jason's aunt Linda and her acquaintances were heavy drug users. He and I were hitting coke and speed pretty hard, but we'd never touch a needle.

They were also major dealers, and Jason was being pulled in with them. I stayed out of the deals and away from the big dealers.

I hinted that we should get married, hoping for permanence and commitment. But Jason had already been down that road and wasn't interested.

Day after day, indistinct anxiety and insecurity grew. Even though rampant chemical abuse around me had created the anxiety, drugs were the only relief I had ever known.

Walking down the aisle of a Kmart one day, I ducked my head only slightly and snorted a line of coke right from a baggie in my purse.

"Who are you?" I said, looking in the mirror later that day. "How did you get here?" Despair washed over me when I had no answer.

Jason and I finally married in September 1984 and moved back to Kalispell.

ಞಞಞ

One month after I arrived in Hoonah, I landed a job with the Forest Service. I didn't plan to stay in Alaska forever, but I had Casey to think of. Jason was spiraling deeper in dealing and using drugs even as I was trying to get away from them.

THE PATH BACK HOME

"Nothing has changed." I confronted him after six months. "You're still spending all your money on drugs and drinking and staying out all night. I can't go on like this. You don't care about me or Casey or even Ben." Jason's 12-year-old son had recently moved up to live with us.

"I *do* care." He turned on the charm. "I love you, Terri, really I do. You are all that matters to me. I promise I'll change."

Emptiness filled my heart. *Is this it? Is this all there is?*

I sat in the back of the little Presbyterian church in Hoonah as I had for several weeks. Unsure of what I hoped to find there, I came because I didn't know what else to do.

"Hi, Virgil. I'm sorry, Jason's not here," I said, answering the door one Sunday afternoon.

"Okay, I'll catch him later. How are you?"

I smiled and stepped back to let him in. He clomped back into the kitchen where he accepted a cup of coffee and leaned against the counter.

Virgil lived up at "The Farm," a camp about seven miles outside of Hoonah. I had no idea of the commune's beliefs, but Virgil was genuinely likable.

"I'm okay. I just got back from church." I stretched to make conversation.

"Hmm." His bushy eyebrows went up. "What are you goin' to church for?"

That's an odd question, I thought. "I don't know. So far, it hasn't really done a lot for me."

SECRETS OF THE WIND

He smiled. "Well, Terri, have you ever asked Jesus into your heart?"

"What are you talking about?" I stared at him. "I went to Sunday school all my life."

"Great. But did you ever ask Jesus into your heart?" he quizzed.

"Well, apparently not," I said simply, "because I have no idea what you're talking about."

"Oh, well, it's really easy. Here, I'll help you." He knelt down and motioned for me to do the same. Then he led me in a prayer to invite Jesus Christ to come into my life and be my Savior.

Jesus had never been a real person to me. Virgil's simple instruction to invite him into my life was difficult to grasp. With interest, though, I took the Bible Virgil gave me and began reading it every time I had a chance.

Some passages carried me back to Sunday school days. Most raised more questions. Even when the words did not make sense, I found they lifted me. I felt as if I was caught up on a gentle breeze.

༺༺༺

"God hates divorce." The text shot from the Holy Bible directly into my heart. For some time, I'd known my marriage was doomed and anticipated divorce. Condemnation swept over me as I translated the statement, *God hates me.*

I slammed the leather-bound volume shut and tossed

THE PATH BACK HOME

it on the shelf. There it sat for months. Occasionally, I'd catch sight of it. My longing to pick it up and draw comfort from its potential truths overcame me, and tears would fill my eyes. But I couldn't bear more rejection from heaven. No more terrifying suggestion could enter my imagination than God's hatred. I swallowed hard and dusted around the oracle in order to avoid its sting.

In the second summer of working for the Forest Service, I began to confide my struggles to a co-worker, Chris. Chris listened for hours as I rattled on about my hopeless marriage. He never gave me advice. He just listened. Before long, it was clear that my marriage was falling apart, and I was falling in love.

The divorce was ugly. We'd both been unfaithful and had plenty of ammunition to unload on each other. Chris and I and Casey moved to Juneau for a few months when it was over.

Habitual infidelity and adultery had become such natural responses that I was tempted at times to cheat on Chris. But Chris was just too kind to hurt. In spite of our perilous beginning and living together outside of marriage, we remained committed and faithful. October of 1991, Chris and I were married.

Life stabilized, as if an agreement had been reached. Like Hoonah's unwritten contract with the earth and ocean, I found a cove where the wind didn't blow quite as hard, and somehow I was hanging on like the houses and the boats.

The three of us moved onto a boat and learned to let

SECRETS OF THE WIND

the sea rock us to sleep at night and wake us gently most mornings.

I decided to take a year off from the Forest Service because I'd worked steadily since Casey was born. We were comfortable and happy.

⇜⇜⇜

"You're going back?" Chris watched as I got up earlier than usual on a Sunday morning in February 1992 and dressed for church. He knew that the previous Sunday was the first time I'd set foot in church since I'd been put off by what I'd read about divorce in the Bible.

"Yeah, well, I liked the music. Since Barb and Kathy are in the band and they both invited me, what can it hurt?" I explained.

Kathy, Casey's kindergarten teacher, was the first to invite me to Abundant Life Christian Fellowship. She played the piano at the church. Later, my friend Barb had said, "Terri, it would be so great if you would come. I play the bass for the worship band, but I'll sit with you during the message."

Worship band? I wondered silently. *Well, I guess "message" is probably like a sermon.*

Out of courtesy and curiosity, I attended.

The worship band played upbeat songs, and the audience spontaneously stood and clapped to the beat. Some people raised their hands like they would at a concert, but they weren't expressing adoration to the

THE PATH BACK HOME

band. Even the band members had their eyes closed, half-singing and half-praying toward heaven. The words of the songs were simpler than the hymns I'd grown up with. I didn't understand everything, but they were clearly love songs reflecting a relationship with Jesus Christ.

Chris' surprise was understandable. The *message* had been delivered by a missionary, and I had related it to Chris when I got home.

"It was disappointing. This missionary guy just got up there and talked about how he wants some money so he can fly his airplane around Brazil. Ya' know, I'd like some money to go fly around South America, too."

We both laughed.

"Maybe the regular preacher will be different," I suggested, and I finished getting ready for the second week.

My amusement when yet another missionary was introduced turned quickly to joyful surprise when he began speaking.

The older gentleman that came to the podium didn't ask for money. He said, "My mission field is in the prisons."

Then he began to relate to us the miracles he had seen happen in the lives of hardened criminals, drug addicts, thieves and thugs. He explained how the real change occurred when each of them had come to know Jesus personally.

Suddenly, the conversation I'd had with Virgil years before made sense. I remembered the prayer I'd repeated

SECRETS OF THE WIND

inviting Jesus into my life. Things I'd memorized as a child came flooding back.

A supernatural presence entered the room, invisible but as real as the thing that woke me in McKelley Hall when I was with the YACC. I wasn't alone this time, and this presence hadn't come uninvited. I realized that the worshipers around me had welcomed Jesus, the living God.

The imposing dark presence that awakened me that horrible night in the dorm had claimed me against my will, surrounding and enclosing me in death. What I was experiencing now was gentle, an awakening within that offered something new, living and hopeful.

The speaker invited anyone who wanted to come forward for prayer. I was compelled but couldn't move. I sat and wept and received the sense of wellbeing and peace that shook me from within.

Strangely reassured that this was not a one-time chance meeting but the beginning of an encounter with supernatural goodness, I hurried from the church.

"Tell me," I insisted as I stood in Barb's doorway. "I don't know what happened to me at church today, and I have to know. I can't describe the relief and power I felt. What was that?"

"Terri, this reminds me of a book I just read," Barb exclaimed. She reached over to an end table, picked up a paperback volume and handed it to me.

As soon as I arrived at home, I began to read the book written by a preacher named Benny Hinn. It described an

THE PATH BACK HOME

experience much like the one I'd had in church. Elated, I discovered what I'd experienced was the power of God coming into my life. And since it had happened to others in similar ways, I realized I'd been radically changed — "born again," made new through Jesus.

ཪ་ཪ་ཪ་

"Jesus said that unless you are born again in the Spirit, you cannot enter the kingdom of God. That which is born of flesh is flesh. That which is born of Spirit is Spirit" (John 3:5).

I went home, and that evening as we prepared to eat dinner, I said, "We have to pray."

Chris and Casey both looked puzzled, but they bowed their heads, and I recited a prayer I remembered from childhood.

Later, I talked to Chris about what had happened to me. A funny look passed over his face, but his normal reserve caused me to dismiss his silence. That night, after we went to bed, I put my hands on him and prayed for him.

Still awake at 2 a.m., a random thought, almost audible and very distinct, passed through my mind: *You need to get that Bible and read it.*

It was a voice, but not a voice. Instinctively, I knew it was God.

What Bible? I wondered, childishly.

You know good and well what Bible.

SECRETS OF THE WIND

He seemed to be smiling as he said it.

The Bible was in our storage shed. *God, there must be 50 boxes in there. I'm not going out there to get it right now.*

At 7 a.m., I tromped out to the shed and dug through several boxes until I found the book I'd tossed on the shelf the day I'd read "God hates divorce."

How could I have thought God hates me? I was so filled with peace and love at the moment that I couldn't fathom the condemnation that crushed me before.

Abundant Life Christian Fellowship affirmed God's love and acceptance, demonstrating it in practical terms. Tena and Debbie, two women from ALCF, took me under their wing and taught me how to pray and study the Bible. They responded to my intense desire to know God by encouraging my pursuit.

I was no longer doing drugs, but I also lost all appetite for alcohol and stopped swearing. Lingering sexual temptations and thoughts that hindered our marriage ceased. Compassion replaced the hurt and bitterness that I felt toward my ex-husband, and I prayed that he would find God.

During a week of special meetings, I became so excited about the grace and power of God that I went straight home to tell my husband.

"Chris! Chris! You've *got* to wake up and talk to me!" Chris rolled over, trying to scrunch the sleep from his eyes. "Honey," I blurted, "I am totally into this Jesus thing. I have to know where you stand."

THE PATH BACK HOME

Silence.

"I love you, and I will never divorce you, but I want you to know this is what I want to do with my life," I continued.

Silence.

Maybe he's not really awake.

My thoughts raced. It wasn't the first time that my straightforward self-expression had left my husband speechless.

"Look, honey," I rushed on, "I just need you to know that this is the way I am going, and I have to know where you stand."

He paused. With absolute resolve and conviction, I'd come to faith in Jesus Christ, and I wanted him to believe, as well. In the recesses of my heart, I also desired his approval.

I took a deep breath and prepared to elaborate my intentions. His wide-open eyes fixed upon mine halted me.

"Terri, I know about this stuff. I grew up with it. I was saved as a kid," he confessed.

I gasped at the revelation. "You *know*?"

"Yes, but listen, honey. I'm not into it like you are. You're excited and that's fine. I've been like that at times myself." He sighed.

Lord, please don't let him reject me for this. I waited breathlessly.

"I accepted Jesus as a kid," he reiterated. "Then I fell away, came back and fell away again."

SECRETS OF THE WIND

Bursting with dozens of questions, I pressed my lips together and held them with my teeth.

"I won't ever leave you, either," he promised. "But don't push this on me. I'm not ready."

Slightly disappointed by the finality in his tone, I nodded slowly. Former fears of abandonment and rejection had been dispelled, either by his words or by the perfect love that I now had inside of me.

"Okay," I said simply.

He reached to kiss me goodnight, and we hugged.

Over the next few weeks, I prayed for Chris. Each time I felt anxious to try to persuade him, God helped me keep silent.

Then one Sunday, just a few months later, Chris came to church. Soon we were growing together. Within the year, we remarried in the church.

༄༄༄

As soon as I received Christ, I wanted to know him and experience him in every way possible and to lead others to him. Immediately, I began to help with youth and children's ministry.

The more I came to know God, the more I came to know myself and the more I wanted to be like him. "The wind blows where it wishes, and you hear the sound of it, but cannot tell where it comes from and where it goes. So it is with everyone born of the Spirit" (John 3:8).

I came to recognize that God's spirit is like a wind. I

THE PATH BACK HOME

could hear it, and I could tell when someone was moved by it, like the rustling leaves on a tree. And I myself could feel and hear him moving daily in my life to change me and make me more like him. But I continued to be wonderfully surprised by the source and the destination.

☙☙☙

"I'm a murderer," the speaker at our Women's Fellowship announced. Stunned, I stared up at her blankly.

"Some of you may know; some do not. But I am a murderer," she continued. "I had an abortion."

Never before had I considered the decision I made as an 18 year old in those terms. Those words deeply impacted me.

☙☙☙

"Terri, I'm going away this weekend," my friend Brenda explained. "My nieces are visiting. Could you watch them for me?"

The oldest one, Natalie, stirred my heart in a special way, and I began to pray for her earnestly.

As I was exercising one day, I began to talk to God about how strongly I was drawn to her. "It's as though she could be my own."

In that still voice, he whispered, "She could be."

Calculating rapidly in my head, I realized Natalie was the exact age as the baby I aborted. Crumbling to the floor,

SECRETS OF THE WIND

I wept in repentance. God swept through to uncover the sin of my past at that moment so that he could heal me.

My heart broke when I admitted the significance of my reckless action and reaction. "I'm so sorry, God," I cried. "Please forgive me."

Immediately, he seemed to scoop me up in his arms and transport me to another place alone with him. He erased my guilt and shame, and he assured me of his forgiveness.

Afterward, I named the baby I had aborted Miranda Rose, because I believed she was a little girl. I had a little ceremony to remember and celebrate her. Mourning the loss, I rejoiced to know we will worship together as a family in heaven.

The same current that brought God's grace and forgiveness over the abortion carried a fresh wind of desire to have more children, especially a daughter. The possibilities of this hope being satisfied I knew were severely reduced. Chris had already had a vasectomy. Nevertheless, my newfound faith, barely six months old, prompted the prayer. The next 10 years tested, proved and refined that faith.

☙☙☙

The shore, the boats and houses grew larger in the distance as we approached Hoonah. I looked down at the toddler in my arms. She was 2½ but weighed only 18 pounds. Her body was limp in sleep, yet I knew it held

THE PATH BACK HOME

little strength even when she was awake. Under the dark brown lids, her eyes were listless and would barely look even to us.

January 18, 2004, a day very much like the gloomy day that Casey and I had arrived, Chris and I brought Halle home to her 4-year-old brother, Manny. Clouds hung everywhere except in my heart. Absent were the apprehension, doubt and sorrow that had accompanied me 17 years earlier. My spirit soared as I reveled in the fulfillment of God's promise that we'd adopt both a daughter and a son from Haiti.

Just about the time Manny and Halle were born in Haiti, I began to hear the wind of God's spirit. I didn't know where it came from or where it was taking us. More than clearly spoken words, a deep concern gripped my heart to pray for the people of Haiti.

The powerful interest seized me as I read a magazine article about a woman in Haiti. For months and years, I prayed for Haiti, chasing every connection that developed and trying to find a way to take a mission trip there. Every plan melted like snowflakes on water.

"God, I give up!" I finally conceded. "God, if all I am to do is to pray for Haiti, then that's what I will do for the rest of my life, even if I never get to go there."

Days after this complete surrender, a letter arrived in my mailbox containing yet another article about ministry in Haiti. Unexpectedly, I acquired the phone number of the woman featured in the article. She'd founded an orphanage in Haiti.

SECRETS OF THE WIND

"Hi. My name is Terri. I'm just a nobody from nowhere. But I want to come to Haiti," I began. Again my enthusiasm was spilling over. I spoke rapidly and directly. "I want to come and stay for three weeks and help you in any way that I can. You just pick the time, and I will come."

"Of course," she said almost immediately.

"Really?" I could hardly believe my ears.

I felt certain Chris was to go with me, but the date coincided with another mission commitment he and his dad had. When that mission was postponed, we were sure God was leading us. Chris, Casey and I all went to Haiti.

That first trip only fueled my burden for Haiti. For weeks, I couldn't think of it without breaking down and crying. The idea of adoption came immediately, but I left it in God's hands to speak to Chris.

As before, I had my thoughts and plans about which children it would be and how the adoption would be arranged. And as it had been with our first trip, returning to Haiti, as well as adopting Manny and Halle, were determined by God's activities, not ours.

꙳꙳꙳

Excruciating pain shot through my knee, and I cried out as I had the day I'd torn my ACL weeks before. That winter day, perfect for sledding, I wound up at the bottom of the hill calling out to my EMT husband, "Help me, Chris! I can't move."

THE PATH BACK HOME

Twenty years in Hoonah taught me to look to God as my primary medical care provider. Prompt to make house calls, I'd found him to be faithful throughout Casey's childhood. Every day we had seen how the Lord was working to restore Halle to a healthy little girl. I believed God was going to heal my knee.

Now I lay flat on my back on the carpet in the little church in which I'd been saved, discipled to follow Christ and mentored in faith. Most incredibly, we had become interim pastors at Abundant Life Christian Fellowship.

The miracles in our lives had been many.

But I was only days away from taking a third mission trip to Haiti, and I couldn't move. I cried out to God, "Help me! I can't go to Haiti like this."

Instead of vanishing, the pain grew fierce, shooting through my knee and bringing tears to my eyes. Chris had to help me home to bed.

Rising the next day, I went to the pool to swim as I had done daily before and since the accident. Unable to kick, I used my arms to drag myself through the water for several slow laps each day, making awkward, choppy turns when I reached the ends of the pool.

Carefully, I stepped down into the pool and swam the length gingerly. Reaching the wall, I did a quick flip, planted my feet squarely and gave myself a vigorous push. Effortlessly gliding under the water, I paused before resuming steady arm strokes.

Then it struck me: *I just bent my knees and pushed off on that turn, and it didn't hurt!*

SECRETS OF THE WIND

    Mischievous delight compelled me to kick my legs as hard as I could. Still I felt no pain. Several smooth, pain-free laps later, I climbed out of the pool and hurried home. I couldn't wait to tell Chris and the kids the latest secret God had sent to us on his gentle wind here in Hoonah.

WARRIOR HEART
The Story of Reggie Butler, Jr.
Written by Ralene Butler

Auntie said the Indian Devil followed me.

She could see him: the blue hazy shape, hovering between my shoulder blades. My aunties looked at me quizzically as I sat down at the kitchen table in Mom and Dad's house. I had just finished drum practice with Dancing Again Singers, a Native group my twin brother and I created when we decided to live an alcohol-free life.

"He's been having *nightmares*," Mom said, with concern in her voice.

My aunties knew, without speaking, that an evil presence was trying, once again, to undermine and attack all I had overcome and accomplished in my young life. This evil presence is called *'uma'ah* by my Yurok ancestors.

They were right: I hated to sleep anymore. At night *'uma'ah* fastened upon me with the intent to harm. I could barely breathe as I fought it while furiously praying.

Make no mistake, there were many battles for my soul, but Gram always said God never gives you more than you can handle. Gram was right.

Here is my story.

☙☙☙

THE PATH BACK HOME

Gram was a Yurok Indian from Northern California, who married my grandpa, a Siletz, from the Oregon coast. Both were full-blooded Indians who served as missionaries in the Indian Shaker church. Gram's pride in her Native American heritage and her love for family and God flowed in my veins; however, I faltered in embracing her faith as I entered adolescence and young adulthood. My family followed Gram's path, but I forged my own path. So did my twin brother, Lee. Gram's path led to God, and my path led to near destruction.

❧❧❧

My childhood was happy and carefree. As a young boy, I spent each summer with Gram, who lived in the "pink house" in Wautek Village, located in the remotest regions of the Yurok reservation — among kerosene lamps (there wasn't electricity) and lots of love.

I loved Gram. She taught us the Indian ways. On the reservation we hunted and fished alongside our uncles and helped Gram gather sticks for basketmaking and huckleberries for pie. Gram also encouraged us to eat seaweed (so we could be strong and healthy) and gently nudged us into choking down acorns (so we could become strong Indian warriors).

"Tie it off! Tie it off!"

My brother, Lee, and I, along with our cousins, swayed back and forth in Uncle's boat as we struggled to set the gill net. Lee grabbed the line with me, grinning, and with

WARRIOR HEART

all the strength skinny 10 year olds could muster, we managed to fling the net into the river — much to our uncle's amazement.

Lee and I gazed at our handiwork with a sense of accomplishment. The gill net billowed amid the Klamath River. We anxiously watched and waited for the tentative bobbing of the float that signals the tangling of gill and fin in the mesh.

Gram, Mom and Auntie canned or smoked the bounty, worth more than silver or gold, brought home by their 10-year-old hunters and gatherers.

Fish smoked the old way is my favorite. Lee and I followed Gram to the smokehouse with strips of fish to be hung from the rafters. Gram told a scary story within the darkened confines of the smokehouse as she briskly started the fire. As we nervously listened to the story, Lee and I eyed the fish that was already smoked and ready to be eaten. We waited in hopeful anticipation of Gram reaching into her apron pocket for the piece of hard bread that would accompany the strips of already smoked fish. The scary story was nearly forgotten as we happily devoured the fish. This was our special moment with Gram.

Religion was extraordinarily important to Gram. She took us to the Indian Shaker church in Wautek Village and in Smith River, California. I used to follow Grandpa around the church, like a little duckling, ringing my bells and stomping my cowboy boots as loudly as possible to the rhythm of the Shakers' melodious harmony. During

THE PATH BACK HOME

the testimonial, I listened raptly as Gram invariably gave God the glory for her many grandchildren.

Gram used Indian parables to instill values in her grandchildren — and the parable was always infused with a gentle reminder to pray to God during trials and tribulations and to shower God with honor, praise and glory during times of triumph. Gram's understanding of Indian tradition, along with her genuine grasp of Christian values, allows me to live as a Native American *and* attend a Christian church.

Sadly, Gram passed before most of my children could feel her comforting embrace, hear her mischievous laughter or see her dance and sing praises to God in the Indian Shaker church. They are, however, listening to *Koochie's* (Yurok for great-grandmother) Indian parables and learning to be virtuous children of God.

ॐॐॐ

Life on the Yurok reservation was a refreshing experience. I learned to live in a society where family is more important than the accumulation of material wealth, and preservation of nature in its pristine state is more important than commercial development. However, the lack of employment on the reservation compelled our family to live in a little coastal town in Oregon where ours was one of three minority families, and our uncle's was another. Our parents gently taught us to co-exist in two societies.

WARRIOR HEART

My twin brother and I were born in Reedsport, Oregon. I never let him forget that I was born 30 minutes ahead of him. I was the boss. Photos taken during our toddler years bear proof of my role as the bossy twin — I always held the toy.

In Reedsport we lived with our parents and sister. Dad was a logger who was as tough as his leather cork boots and steely as his tin hat. He spent most of his young life working the logging camps from Northern California to Alaska. In his mid-30s he married a beautiful Indian girl, my mom, and they settled down in Reedsport. Every evening, right before dinner, we waited on the front porch for the *crummy* (van transporting loggers to and from the work site) to arrive. We knew Dad always kept a bit of his lunch — usually the sweets — for us. Dad worked as a logger until he was 62 years old. He often said our "hungry little eyes" kept him motivated to awaken at 4:30 in the morning to work, rain or shine, in a physically demanding job.

Mom was a gentle yet determined woman who wanted her children to live their dreams — for with God on our side, what couldn't we accomplish? She worked first at a fish cannery and then for the school district in Reedsport, while attending college and raising three very spoiled children. Mom loved the Assemblies of God church. She dressed us in matching outfits (of different colors) every Sunday when we attended Sunday school and "big people church," and she drove us to youth group every Tuesday so we could participate in Buckaroos and then Royal

THE PATH BACK HOME

Rangers. Mom instilled within us a sense of values that I now share with my children — to live a virtuous life. Finally, and most importantly, Mom always quotes Philippians 4:13 when a chapter in our life starts and ends or when the light at the end of the tunnel is but a faint flicker: "I can do all things through Christ which strengtheneth me" (KJV).

❧❧❧

As adolescence loomed on the horizon, we moved to the "old house" in Siletz, Oregon. The house, rundown and dilapidated in appearance, was rich in memories. Our family readily and happily embraced this new adventure.

The house was in need of rehabilitation. No paint outside. No water heater inside. The curtains ruffled in breezes even if the doors were closed. The walls had no insulation, and the builder must have had a sense of humor: He constructed the privy one mad dash out the back door and a few steps across the porch. Bathing would be an ordeal: Mom would have to heat bathwater over a stove! In the massive kitchen, a bed sat majestically in the corner.

Siletz's "urban center" was just a stroll away from our front porch: Bensell's Store, a mercantile supplying all kinds of groceries and sundries; a couple restaurants (one with a bar for rowdy loggers attached); two gas stations; a U.S. Post Office; and the Siletz City Hall.

Mom found a job with the Bureau of Indian Affairs.

WARRIOR HEART

Most parents of my new friends at school worked in lumber mills or for logging companies. Several worked in Toledo, about nine miles south of Siletz, at a massive paper mill.

Mom enrolled my brother and me for sixth grade at the Siletz Valley School. My older sister attended high school in the same building, much to her dismay.

☙☙☙

We stoically listened to their taunts. Lee and I stood back to back as the bigger boys closed in.

We were the new kids in school, and we had never fought before. Our life in Reedsport had been fairly idyllic, surrounded by close family and members of our church. The Reedsport schools were known for academic success and discipline rather than for student fighting and bullying.

The students were a couple of grades ahead of us at Siletz Elementary School, and they thought we would run from a beating. They lunged at us with curses spewing and fists flying. When the ordeal ended, we were bruised but unharmed.

About two thirds of our new school was non-native. Our first year was fairly peaceful, except for the usual "unnecessary roughness" in football or basketball. Only a few classmates challenged us to fistfights. But by the eighth grade, hardly a week went by that we didn't mix it up with the same group of older students. A reputation

THE PATH BACK HOME

fastened on us among the bullies in school — fight one Butler twin and you ended up fighting the other and probably *both* at the same time when you didn't expect it.

Attendance at Siletz Elementary School was hardly the ideal academic experience. However, other pursuits created fond childhood memories. Baseball, basketball, football and wrestling practice encompassed most of my free time. The weekends were devoted to racing around town and on the logging roads on my dirt bike, fishing, hunting and learning the ways of the Siletz.

I danced like a warrior with other young men and women of the Confederated Tribes of Siletz at the *Nesika Illahee* ("Our Land") Powwow. It set my heart aflame with pride to learn the dances the Indian warriors passed down from generation to generation and to follow the guidance of my elders in creating the traditional regalia.

Sunday mornings were hectic, but Mom always made sure we attended Sunday school at the Siletz Gospel Tabernacle, an Assemblies of God church like the one we had attended in Reedsport. I heard the good words about Jesus, but as I careened through adolescence, the whole religious thing seemed like fishing without bait: I had no expectation of really catching anything.

˜˜˜

As Lee and I were on the threshold of sauntering a few steps (literally) west to Siletz High, home of the mighty Warriors, the district closed the school after a heroic

WARRIOR HEART

battle, mounted by the parents (my mom included), ended in defeat. So as a freshman I found myself walking the hallowed halls of Toledo High School where many of the students were sons and daughters of local millworkers.

At Toledo High, it was hard to feel accepted by the cliques that had been in existence there since elementary school or by the teachers who devoted their careers to cultivating the academic success of Toledo students. The culture clash between the Siletz and Toledo students was inevitable — it was neither their fault nor ours. Although this was far from an ideal academic experience, there was a saving grace: Lee and I met a Toledo student who became a brother to us and, later, an uncle to our children. Our friend's support during life's many trials and tribulations has been unwavering. He has never stood in judgment, and when the dust settled from the latest skirmish, he was usually sitting, quite comfortable, by our side.

༄༄༄

We would both graduate from Toledo soon, and Mom was determined to see her sons grace the academic halls of Oregon State University.

She spread the applications on the kitchen table, bright brochures with lots of courses to choose from — weight lifting, physical education ...

We were accepted! Soon, two very sheltered and spoiled Indian boys from Siletz, Oregon, would swim

THE PATH BACK HOME

among the academic sharks at OSU like salmon in a big, challenging and treacherous sea.

Dorm life at Oregon State University suited Lee and me. We were liberated, or so we thought, to live our lives our way — with Mom and Dad paying the bills, of course. We enrolled in the Educational Opportunities Program, which provided assistance with admissions, orientation, academic and personal advising, tutoring and finding internships and jobs. We also joined a Native American club to learn about the traditions of other Indian tribes and developed friendships with foreign students whose families sacrificed to send them to OSU.

We twins were 18 years old, and the world was our oyster for a while. Freshman year we were bewildered at the breakneck pace of the world around us; however, we managed to study, attend classes and build friendships.

In our sophomore year, we discovered college parties where alcohol flowed in torrents amid the now treacherous sea. We cut so many classes that the professors finally dropped us. By Christmas, Mom's hope for us to gain forestry careers took second place to our need to overcome the demons that accompany emerging alcohol dependency.

During sober moments, I realized that I teetered on the edge of full-tilt addiction to alcohol. One day Lee and I simply packed up and moved home to Siletz. Dad didn't say much, but I knew he was watching his own mistakes reflected in his sons.

WARRIOR HEART

☙☙☙

At home, a horrific and tragic event literally shook my world.

Lee and I worked seasonal jobs for the United States Forest Service as firefighters. We lived in Walport, Oregon, during the firefighting season. One day, we received an urgent message to come home immediately.

"It's your cousin William, boys," Mom said, wiping tears from her eyes. "He was killed in a car accident. He's gone."

Will was like a little brother, I said to myself, barely comprehending her words. Will, Lee and I had raced around Wautek Village every summer as children. We swam all day, hiked in the forest, shot our BB guns — Gram said whatever you kill, you eat, even if it's a slug — and rode wild horses, until we heard Auntie's whistle signaling time to return home.

"How'd it happen?" Lee asked.

Mom fixed her gaze upon our grief-stricken countenances. "Driving *drunk*," she said.

I still grieve for my "little brother." Sadly, his death did not catapult me into sobriety. Rather, I drank more than ever. It would take a near brush with prison to shake my world, again.

☙☙☙

"Is that the house?"

"Yeah. That's it." My cousin unconsciously ran a hand

THE PATH BACK HOME

over his swollen face, still smarting from the severe beating he took a few days before. I placed a hand on his shoulder.

"I'm okay," he said.

Lee and I were seething. These menaces to society beat our cousin. We sat in the car for a while, watching the windows of the house while sipping beer. There were four of us.

Suddenly we threw open the car doors and lunged out, fully prepared to avenge our cousin's honor. The door to the house gave way easily, but the three big men inside had weapons ready.

After the beat down, we stumbled to our car, slashed, battered and bloody. Sometime later someone must have called the Oregon State Police.

I awoke the following morning, stiff, guilty and repentant. In the shower, I fingered an open wound on my scalp and groaned while blood painted swirls around the shower drain. Someone had clubbed me, though I didn't recall who.

I had barely dressed before two Oregon State troopers knocked on the door.

Over the following months, my assault charge crept slowly through the halls of justice. Weapons were involved, and the prosecutor could have saddled me with attempted murder. At the time, Mom and others in my family were praying for Lee and me, but little gratitude seeped past my big ego. What did leak out of this ugliness was my first sustained attempt at sobriety. The district attorney asked my mom's opinion about the appropriate punishment, and she suggested attendance at a rehabilitation facility. So it was that I was forced to sign up for AA (Alcoholics Anonymous) and drug and alcohol counseling.

༄༄༄

Lee was ready to be rehabilitated, but I dragged my feet at first. With his encouragement, I finally registered at a Native American drug and alcohol treatment center. The center targeted specific concerns common to Indians, and I learned how to control my addiction, bit by bit. I finished the court-mandated treatment program and continued attending meetings for months afterward. I truly believed that my meetings with other addicts for moral support, along with continued therapy, would keep me on the path of healing.

Lee moved to the Grand Ronde reservation in Northwest Oregon, and I stayed at Dad and Mom's home, trying to stay sober, working part-time for the tribe and doing odd jobs for the forestry department. I tried to go back to college again for a time, but the old cravings surreptitiously emerged — I actually believed that I could drink on the weekends, just a little.

I had been part of a drum group, on and off, since my early 20s. I had often drummed at schools and at our annual *Nesika Illahee* ("Our Land") Powwow in Siletz. Now my heritage called me back, and I rejoined a drum

THE PATH BACK HOME

group, hoping to recapture some of my old happiness and maintain my sobriety.

All my addiction therapies failed. And as for my deeply rooted Indian heritage: It satisfied my pride, *but it could not save my soul.*

In fewer than 10 months after drug and alcohol therapy, I was drinking again. Night after night, I lay in an abyss of depression where the nightmares reigned supreme.

☙☙☙

Beer made me feel invincible, but not today. I slouched in the back of my pickup truck, slamming beer with Lee, pondering the death of Gram.

Auntie had warned us, "You boys better start learning to pray for yourselves. Your gram has spent many hours on her knees interceding to God for you, but she's gone now."

I tossed the can in the truck bed with a few other empties. "Gram was a powerful Christian, ya know? She always knew when I was in trouble."

Lee looked thoughtful. "Yeah, she always knew — and prayed for us."

Gram loved her grandchildren more than life itself. I was glad that Gram was in heaven; however, the mere thought of life without her was unbearable. I also couldn't help but wonder, *Who has the patience and perseverance to pray for me like Gram did?*

WARRIOR HEART

I never really stopped praying. It was one teaching I absorbed and retained from years of Sunday school and the teachings of Gram and Mom. When I prayed, however, I was merely reciting words learned in Sunday school. With Gram's passing, I understood life's fragility; so, with a broken heart, I prayed as never before. I prayed for my family and for my life. And my reliance upon alcohol started to wane.

༄༄༄

I was in my early 20s when Auntie, my mom and their friends joined hands and prayed for me in Mom's kitchen. When they ordered the Indian Devil to leave, it did, and my nightmares vanished, too.

Afterward, their continued faithful prayers pointed God's mercy straight at my heart. And God waited patiently as I struggled to overcome my demons so he could provide the abundant life. What God planned for my future was beyond my wildest dreams: a beautiful drum group of Butlers, yet unborn, waiting for me to lead them in new songs.

༄༄༄

My brother's new wife introduced me to Melinda, a woman I fell in love with. We started a family — the "logical" path for a 30-something Indian man who had finished sowing his wild oats. My greatest accomplishments in life are the birth of my five children.

THE PATH BACK HOME

My path to salvation started with the birth of my first child. And I hit the final bump in my path shortly before the birth of my second child — a beautiful baby girl.

It was about family honor again at a tribal gathering, and others joined me as I handled an insult with my fists. Battered, but still standing (before a judge), I was a hair's breadth away from losing my freedom, perhaps for years.

"You're about to throw your life away, Reggie."

My mom and dad had suffered greatly from my lack of judgment over the years, and this time my lengthy court case haunted them. They helped with legal costs and babysat while I appeared for court proceedings. One day when I picked up the kids, Mom's dark eyes bored into me. From heaven, it seemed like Gram watched me, too.

"I remember you and Lee in the Christmas plays," Mom said. "You played angels and wise men at different times. You remember how proud Dad and I were, watching our sons?"

I nodded and took a deep breath, wishing I didn't.

"I love you, Reggie. I pray for you. But, son, if you keep fighting, you'll never see your kids in Christmas or Easter plays — you'll be in prison."

Her words affected me more than I let on. My eyes teared up, and I turned away.

"Please come to church with me."

I nodded and went home to tell Melinda, "We need to get the kids ready for Sunday school this weekend."

I sat with my family at Siletz Gospel Tabernacle, the church I had rejected since boyhood, and my past life

WARRIOR HEART

drummed in my mind relentlessly during the pastor's sermon.

I had hurt my family, most importantly, my little son and baby daughter. How could I expect Jesus to accept me?

But another voice in my heart thundered: *Your family believes you are worth saving, and so do I.*

Suddenly, like sunshine cresting a mountain, light fell on a path I never expected to see. It was Gram's path, and I stood up.

It was a long march to the front of my church where everyone knew me. I could barely breathe by the time I got to the altar.

"I need Jesus," I said simply, and the pastor told me to talk directly to God.

I knelt right there and poured out my soul, broken up and bitter over my bad decisions. As I prayed, I felt heaps of guilt, anger and even my desire for alcohol melt off me like afternoon dew.

In my spirit, Jesus told me that he loved me. He forgave me for squandering my precious youth, and I humbly committed the rest of my time on earth to him. My ancestors would always be an important part of my traditions, but my worship belonged to Jesus Christ. I craved to know Gram's God and beloved friend.

Melinda committed her life to Jesus, too, a matter of days after I did. And so did Lee.

Because of God's mercy, I escaped from a prison sentence a second time.

THE PATH BACK HOME

Sadly, an agony of another sort awaited me. Yet my faith grew stronger as I braced against an emotional hurricane I could never have forecast.

☙☙☙

My son Jonathan died of SIDS (sudden infant death syndrome) at 4 months old. The birth of my triplets (the trips) was a wondrous event.

Jonathan was the healthiest of my three babies, who were born premature and with numerous health problems. The trips were community babies — each day someone from the church or tribe would drop by the house to lend a hand, since Melinda and I were raising five babies under 5 years old.

I will always feel a twinge of sorrow thinking about my son. I wonder if he'd like wrestling and football — his brother doesn't — or if he would enjoy drawing, like his sister.

God's comforting embrace is the reason I survived my baby's death.

☙☙☙

A wall of overwhelming loss grew between Melinda and me, and we grieved for Jonathan in separate ways. Over the years our marriage grew thin as springtime ice, and one day the *trust* between us shattered to pieces.

Our house turned into a battleground, and we separated.

WARRIOR HEART

Melinda found a new person to share her life with, while I reached out to family and friends at Siletz Gospel Tabernacle. The church family, along with my mom, dad, brother and sister, were a soothing balm as I struggled with the demise of my marriage and the potential loss of my children.

Pastor Vance counseled me to forgive and let go of the bitterness as the prolonged divorce and custody hearings raged relentlessly on, but my heart was torn. I felt as if I lost my Jonathan only yesterday, though years had passed. I felt empty and alone, especially as I feared losing Jonathan's brothers and sisters.

These were the darkest days of my life. During this unexpected storm, Jesus gripped my shoulders *hard*, guiding me toward a fully restored life — a life I never imagined possible.

సౌసౌసౌ

I knew Heather from church. I was searching for friendship as we walked on the beach one evening. We discovered that we had much in common: She was Siletz, and so was I; she was a Christian and had attended Siletz Gospel Tabernacle since her childhood, and so had I; she had three children, I had five; she was a single mom, I was a single dad.

After a few months, our relationship progressed from friendship to love. As people in love are prone to do, we grew impatient and yielded to our emotional desires. As a result, my divorce and custody battle raged as we blended our families: Two adults and seven children suddenly shared a four-bedroom home.

If we had sought counsel from Christian friends and our pastor or pondered God's wonderful design for our families, we would have waited before moving in together. Our regret to this day is that our lives sent the wrong message about the sacredness of marriage to our children and other young people in our community.

We are thankful that God's mercy knows no bounds.

One day Heather and I awoke to a Voice playing clearly, like drums on a lake at daybreak. We decided to start over completely.

"Pastor Vance, we would like you to perform our wedding at Siletz Gospel Tabernacle." Heather and I committed our children and future to God, and he has blessed us with the inner strength we needed to live each day as a faithful husband and wife.

And miracles are happening.

I have sole custody of my children, and my grief over Jonathan has turned to special compassion for those who have lost loved ones. The "why" question seldom breaks through my solid assurance that Jonathan lives in a place where death and pain do not exist. He is well and happy with Jesus in heaven.

Meanwhile, here on earth, the Butlers are dancing again to the music of God's grace, led by the heart of a warrior.

HAND ON MY HEART
The Story of Pamela Lane
Written by Jessica Boling

Screech! Crash!

I was driving down a hill in Toledo, Oregon, when my car spun out of control and careened into the back of a parked car. Dazed, confused and uncertain of my surroundings, I awoke from my momentary unconscious state. Slowly I used every sore muscle in my neck to peer over my steering wheel through a battered windshield at the parked car before me. I hopped out of the car for a closer view.

"Are you all right?" a man yelled from a nearby apartment building window.

I couldn't stop staring at the damage.

"No," I managed, "I'm not." I paused. "I'm drunk, and I rear ended this parked car."

I started walking toward the stranger, who was standing nearly 20 feet away.

"You're in trouble," he warned, shaking his head.

"Yes," I said. "I know."

From a distance, I heard police sirens scream closer and closer. An officer soon jumped out of a patrol car and surveyed the situation. After questioning me, he said, "I'm citing you for driving under the influence of alcohol."

Panic rose in my chest. "Please take me to jail," I begged. "Please. I don't want my family to be involved."

THE PATH BACK HOME

I thought of my mother and cringed. She was in Siletz, Oregon, with three of my five children.

How did I get here? I wondered. It was 1987, and I was 39 years old. Looking back, I realize that the DUI was the climax of a series of events and decisions that had become the fabric of my life.

☙☙☙

I was born in Salem, Oregon, and was a member of the Confederated Tribes of Siletz Indians. The Oregon Coast was a beautiful place, with green landscapes and beautiful ocean views. The sea was never far away, but I lived in the Willamette Valley for most of my life and missed cars, city buses and, most of all, the people I grew up with.

My parents split up when I was a child, and for a few years I lived with my father, along with my three siblings. Then one day he remarried, and we lived with his new wife and her two daughters.

When I was in the eighth grade, my siblings and I moved with our mother and stepfather. We had a fine home, and we all graduated from high school.

At age 21, I, too, got married. Five years and three children later, I left my husband. More children arrived out of wedlock, and by the mid-1980s, I was a single mom struggling to support five children. I decided to pursue college, but with young children to care for, I made slow progress.

In 1986, after three years of pursuing a degree, I

HAND ON MY HEART

received my medical transcription certificate. The signed, stamped document promised freedom and the chance to provide for my children. I resolved to find a job.

I searched with the tribe in Siletz, hoping to find a position. Several times I applied for jobs. There was competition within the tribe, and there were many qualified people vying for one position. My hope rose like an eagle in flight, only to fall to the ground when I was notified that I wasn't the chosen applicant. My spirits sank a bit lower when I couldn't find a position at all. Financially, I was in trouble. I had five children and no husband to help support them, so I turned to the government for assistance. Defeated and depressed, I remained on welfare to keep my family together. My welfare check was just enough to pay for my house rental. There was nothing left for the electric service, let alone cable TV for the children or a telephone.

In the midst of my financial turmoil, my sister dropped by. She took one look at me and knew just the answer to relieve my stress.

"Pam, come to the tavern with me," she urged. "Take some time for yourself, and relax for a while."

I did.

Only I was so drunk when I returned that I had to drive across the street to my sister's house to pick up the kids.

Upon leaving, I backed up a little too much to the right and landed one of my tires in a ditch by the driveway. Struggling with the wheel myself, I asked my son to back

THE PATH BACK HOME

the car out for me — only he then ran over my foot.

But that didn't stop me from putting myself under the influence of judgment-impeding alcohol yet again.

Soon, my stress spurred my depression, and my depression spurred my drinking. I found myself drinking nearly every day. Drinking provided the escape I needed from a life with big demands.

Do I even care if I die? I wondered.

I combated this question with more and more alcohol. And then one night, after only a couple of drinks, the alcohol led me down a hill in Toledo and into a parked car.

ঌঌঌ

The detox center director suggested that I attend a treatment center instead of going to jail, since the DUI was my first offense. I agreed to move to Red Willow, a Native Indian treatment center in Gervais. There I began a 12-step program to rid myself of alcohol addiction.

Red Willow's meetings were filled with Native Americans, old and young, men and women, tugging at the invisible chains of alcohol. Many of the people were longtime alcoholics, buried far deeper in the addiction than I was.

Some stayed, but many ran away — back to life on the streets, existing from one drink to the next. We received a good education on the effects of alcohol and what it does to your body. Learning about the physiological and

HAND ON MY HEART

psychological effects and what alcohol consumption does to your body was an eye opener. I stayed in treatment for five months.

One day, I told a counselor my story.

"Hmm," he responded, catching and holding my gaze with piercing eyes. "We can get ugly, can't we?"

I felt a connection with his words. They were true. He wasn't calling *me* ugly, but pointing out that some of my decisions and actions were mistaken. Wrong.

The counselor wasn't scolding me; he was highlighting something I needed to know: that I was capable of bad choices. Perhaps I was also capable of good choices.

As my group studied the 12 steps, repeating and memorizing the words, I noticed that many of the phrases mentioned God. I'd grown up in church, but had not thought seriously about God for a long time.

During a meeting, one of the counselors explained that God was the "higher power" needed to defeat a drinking addiction.

A young man raised his hand. "I'm not religious," he said. "Can I use something else as my higher power?"

A murmur of voices agreed with the man. The counselor shrugged and agreed that they could substitute another object in place of God. "Whatever helps you," he said. "Use that."

Twisting uneasily in my chair, I considered. *Why did I care what other people thought of God? What did I think of him?* I hadn't been to church for years, but somehow I knew I needed God as my higher power. If I was going to

THE PATH BACK HOME

change, I needed help from something outside myself. I'd tried everything to make my life work, and I'd failed.

Church doors beckoned to me again. I completed the assigned treatment at Red Willow and continued to attend church, study the Bible and try to make good decisions. I began to pray regularly, and it seemed to work. I prayed for a husband, and I met a man in 1989. We both felt we were right for each other, but we weren't. I had a child with him before we split up in 1990.

Again a single mother, this time with a newborn, I allowed discouragement to take me back to the tavern. The disastrous relationship seemed to confirm a suspicion that I was stuck in a pattern and could not change — at least not by myself. I drank, and it felt very defeating to drink after maintaining a couple years of sobriety.

Then I panicked. Was I relapsing? Would alcohol tear me away from my baby son, from my life? I went to a professional counselor to hear his opinion.

"You haven't relapsed," he concluded after hearing my story. "It was only a short time. You've merely had a slip."

"A slip?" I breathed a sigh of relief. When I closed my eyes, I saw the twisted metal bumper of the car I'd rear ended three years earlier. This was another opportunity to wake up. And I did.

If I wanted to change, I had to rely on my higher power. I couldn't fix anything by myself. I knew — I had tried. I needed something bigger. Something stronger. Something that didn't depend on human foibles and emotions. I needed Jesus.

HAND ON MY HEART

I renewed my commitment to church. Now that I held a full-time job in Salem, it was difficult to find time to be involved at church as much as I wanted. But I forced myself to go.

My older children were too independent to come along, but I dragged my son Mark, then 3 years old, with me. On Wednesday nights, we attended prayer meetings at the People's Church, sprinting to catch the last bus after services concluded at 7:30 p.m.

Mark's short legs and small body couldn't always carry him quickly enough, and I grew impatient with his lagging. One night, he sat down on the sidewalk.

"Mark, come on!" I urged, tugging at his arm. "We have to catch the bus. A taxi will cost $20, and I don't have that much. Come on, hurry!"

He just sat there on the sidewalk with both little legs sticking straight out, and I either had to pack him or talk him into running with me to make the bus downtown to catch the last bus to our home across town. It was a time of high stress when he and I both became tired and weary running to the bus stop.

The following Wednesday, we were back at church. I watched the elders standing at the front of the auditorium, holding bottles of oil. They touched fingers to oil and oil to foreheads as they prayed for people who came forward. My knees felt wobbly as I stood up, but something told me I needed to go.

When I reached the front of the room, a female elder approached me. Her eyes searched my face. She seemed to

THE PATH BACK HOME

see past the veneer of my complacent expression to the frayed nerves, exhaustion and hopelessness inside.

She touched her fingers to the oil in the bottle and reached out to my forehead.

"Lord, please restore her mind to her," she prayed.

The woman continued to pray as I stood with my eyes closed, considering what she said. Somehow, she knew what was bothering me without having to ask. As I listened and considered, I recognized that what she prayed was exactly what needed to happen. Mark and I were worn out running from bus stop to bus stop. He was small and needed a break. Without even knowing me, this woman somehow knew my story.

I quit my job and stayed home with Mark for eight months until we found a daycare close to our neighborhood so he wouldn't have to rush back and forth across town. The elder lady's prayer helped me in the decision to quit my job and care for Mark at home for those eight months. Yes, my mind was being restored. Not running to three buses every morning and evening was bringing my thinking process back to normal. Things were looking up when we found his new daycare and preschool in our neighborhood. Had that elder not prayed those exact words for me, I may have continued a hairy routine that was leading my family down a path of total mental and physical exhaustion.

೨೨೨

HAND ON MY HEART

I didn't have a car, and the buses didn't run on Sundays, so I started watching Christian TV instead of attending church. Although I missed talking to real people about God, I learned a lot about the Bible.

My teenage daughter lived with me at the time. Enticed by her friends and the mystery of what might happen, she began to make Ouija boards and hold séances in her bedroom. She dressed in alternative clothing, big and baggy in nature colors, and kept to herself, the bedroom door closed behind her. I feared for her and felt distant from her and depressed as I watched her tread deeper and deeper into the occult world.

As I talked to my mom one day, she expressed concern about my daughter.

"I'm worried about her."

"So am I, Mom."

There was a pause. "Maybe she could come live with me and go to the Christian school again down here in California."

"Maybe." I felt overwhelmed with gratitude and soon agreed to the plan. My daughter moved in with her grandmother and began attending a school where she made new friends and stopped dabbling in the occult.

After she moved, though, I kept her bedroom door closed. Still I felt a presence in my house — a heavy darkness when I walked up the stairs to the bathroom in our townhouse apartment. I was afraid to step foot in her bedroom or even to go up the stairs to the second floor of my townhouse, even though I did it every night.

THE PATH BACK HOME

One evening, I was viewing a program on the Christian TV station. The hosts said if you pray in the name of Jesus, he will answer. Impressively, these church people seemed to believe what they claimed.

Can I believe, too? I wondered.

I decided to try. I believed in God and in his son, Jesus. So I decided to pray in the *name* of Jesus.

My daughter's bedroom door always remained closed. One night, I lay in my bed, and the whole view from my bed facing the hallway was creepy and mysterious. Something seemed dark, and I could almost see a vision of something lurking there in the distance. I said in my prayer out loud with meaning, "Evil spirit, you must leave this house in the name of Jesus. Now leave." I immediately peered down the hallway, and it now seemed lit, even from the total darkness in my room, where I had no light turned on. My bedroom was lighter, and I could see the reflection of the leaves on my wall from the tree outside. The whole upstairs immediately took on a different feeling. The darkness, whatever it was, had left. I thanked God, closed my eyes and slept like the newborn babies I had raised all my life.

Courage now surged through me. I sensed that Jesus was more powerful than any other force, and the realization gave me hope. I wanted to know more. I wanted to know him.

Over the next few years, I continued to pray, read the Bible and watch Christian TV. Eventually, my responsibilities lightened so that I could attend church

HAND ON MY HEART

again. I looked for God, and I found him. I realized that getting to know him was no different from getting to know another person: The more time I spent with him, the better I knew him. There was always more to learn. And he always had more to give.

In 1999, I decided to quit smoking. I felt divided, wanting to serve God but held firm in the grip of a destructive habit. After several attempts to quit, I called a prayer help line in desperation.

"Please pray that I can quit smoking," I told the woman who answered. "I feel like a hypocrite, but I can't stop. I'll even pull the cigarettes I just placed in the garbage can out of the garbage just to smoke one because I can't seem to quit this horrible habit."

"All right." She quoted Philippians 4:13, a verse from the Bible I had been reading so frequently: "I can do all things through Christ who strengthens me." Then she prayed, "Lord, every time Pam smokes a cigarette, make her sick." I agreed with her small and direct prayer, even the sick part. I was serious with this; I didn't want something between me and God, and I wanted to be tobacco free.

The next time I smoked a cigarette, my face puffed and swelled. My stomach rolled with nausea. I physically could not stand the sensation I had enjoyed for so many years. I never smoked after that. Again I felt in awe of the power of Jesus to answer prayers, and I wondered what he would do next.

A year later, I bought a house from tribal housing at

THE PATH BACK HOME

Oak Flats. My mother lived nearby, and my sister Janice moved in with her. It was pleasant to have family so near. Mark could spend time with his grandmother, and I enjoyed the frequent trips back and forth between the two houses. Janice lived with Mom, and they had the good pleasure of attending church together.

One day I stopped by my mom's house to get something and walked into the living room. Mom was on the couch, and Janice was sitting in the recliner, reading aloud. To my amazement, the book spread open on her lap was a black leather Bible.

Mom looked up, smiled and said, "Janice is reading me the gospel of John."

Janice put the Bible down and stood up. She smiled warmly as she came forward to embrace me.

"Pam, I went to church today. You know, I don't want to miss church, I really love going. Where were you? You missed a tremendous service; it was wonderful."

I hugged her. She always hugged so hard and always told me she loved me when she hugged me. As I studied her face, I saw new sparks of life in her dark eyes. She was happily running around the house getting ready for work the next day by the time I left. Before I left, she whispered in my ear, "Come check on Mom tomorrow for lunch. I have to take a friend to the doctor in Portland and then go to Salem. Be back around 4:30."

Then she smiled and left, keys jingling in her wake.

HAND ON MY HEART

It seemed that I had never been happier. Mom, Janice and I all went to Siletz Gospel Tabernacle, the church we had attended when we were little. It seemed that Janice's and my lives had come full circle, and again I was eager to see what God would do next.

Then, the next day, Janice was driving home from Salem, and a storm hit parts of Oregon. High winds and snow fell and struck a narrow mountain pass near Siletz. Janice's car had no traction on the snowy road. As she drove down the mountain, her car slipped out of control. A pickup truck rounded the corner at that moment, and it struck her broadside.

Janice went home to be with the Lord that day.

I was devastated. Grief fell like a tremendous weight, pinning me to the ground. I was so grieved that the depression continued for months. Mom grieved, too, but I felt that I should be stronger. Instead, I was weak, and the pain remained raw. Anxiety overwhelmed me, and I was afraid to stay alone in my room at night. Mom spent the night with me sometimes. Other times, my granddaughter came. It was tempting to distrust God, to ask him, "Why?" But instead, I decided to ask him to comfort me.

He did.

One night, I was driving to Portland. The three-hour drive stretched endlessly. Anxiety gnawed at my insides as I drove over a coastal mountain range. Surrounded by tall trees and a stormy dark night, I navigated the narrow road. It was pitch dark, and I strained to see through the rainy windblown scene. My hands tingled, and my heart

THE PATH BACK HOME

raced. I was overwhelmed with anxieties that were causing me rapid palpitations.

"God," I cried out loud. "Help me!"

Clutching the steering wheel, in need of confirmation that the Lord was listening, I cried out in desperation.

"Jesus, please! If you really exist, I need to know you're with me." Tears poured from my eyes.

I stretched my right hand toward the passenger side of the seat, grasping, like a child, for anything that might comfort me.

"Jesus," I pleaded again, "just give me a sign you are with me because I am so alone!"

A soft, inaudible voice answered. "Pam, put your hand on your heart. That is where I am — in your heart — and I will never leave you."

The comfort of that calm, direct voice broke the spell of panic. I could breathe again. My muscles relaxed. For the rest of the drive home, I sang song after song of praise to Jesus. I knew he was real, and he was with me, and I sang all the way to Portland, for more than two hours on the road.

The God of the universe was with me. He was always with me.

Weeks after my sister's accident, my elderly grandmother passed away from pneumonia. Losing her was difficult, but I knew Gramma was in heaven, too — the same place I knew Janice now dwelled. And that voice and those invisible hands that had been near to me during that scary night drive somehow now wrapped me in peace.

HAND ON MY HEART

You are with me, I thought, hands on my heart. *With me.*

Before, alcohol, people and a sense of financial fear could disturb my peace. Now even death could not shatter that. I had found a fresh calmness and closeness with the Lord to carry me through those times. Just as he did with my car that day in Toledo, God had steered me through collision after collision to lead me to a better route.

And if ever on the journey together I needed the security of knowing I wasn't driving alone, I could remember that night on the Van Duzer Corridor and place my hand over my heart. Jesus is real, and he lives in my heart.

LOVE STORY
The Story of Rocky and Cathy Pavey
Written by Karen Koczwara

Once upon a time.

It's how most love stories start, isn't it?

Perhaps the story begins with a shy glance, a shared laugh, an awkward moment, a smile.

Then there's the middle part, the ups and the downs, the uncertainty, the heroes and villains, the question of whether or not love will stand the test of time.

And then there's the end. *Happily ever after*, as some fairytales read.

Our story began like all the rest, but it's the middle part you need to know about.

The middle part is full of tears, laughter, hope and despair. There were moments when I, Rocky, wondered if it might be the end. Moments when I could not see beyond that hospital room, the doctors' sullen faces and the dark, quiet mornings that bled into dark, quiet nights. Moments when I thought the tears would never stop.

But even then, I held out hope for the happily ever after. I had to believe in tomorrow.

This is our love story.

༺༻༺༻༺༻

THE PATH BACK HOME

"And now, folks, for the limbo contest!" the DJ announced.

The pretty brunette next to me smiled. "You gonna try it?" she asked.

"Sure, why not? But you go first," I replied, laughing. It was hard not to stare at her … big brown eyes, gorgeous smile, long brunette hair that danced along with her to the music in the club. Our friends introduced her as Cathy, and I quickly took note of her name. I never forgot a pretty girl's name.

"Oh, I don't know if I can go that low!" Cathy laughed as she arched her back and ducked under the limbo stick.

"You're a pro!" I cheered her on. "And you're gonna make me look like a fool."

By the end of the night, I wound up with a crick in my neck and a phone number in my pocket. It was just days before Christmas 1989, and winter held its usual chill in Fairbanks, Alaska. Yet Cathy and I were just getting warmed up.

At 26 years old, I was still holding out for Ms. Right. Cathy was a single mother; I quickly grew fond of her 9-year-old son, David. Cathy explained they were a "package deal," and I couldn't have been happier. When I asked her to marry me, she eagerly accepted.

Cathy and I desired more children after we wed, but we were devastated when she got pregnant and miscarried.

"We'll try again," I assured her. "We have plenty of time." Cathy got pregnant three more times, but each pregnancy resulted in a miscarriage. After losing a baby

LOVE STORY

six months into the pregnancy, the heartache was too great. We had tossed around names, shopped for little clothes and discussed paint colors for the nursery. Through many tears, we chose to accept that we were not meant to have more children and focused on David, our wonderful son.

David loved all things motorized, including motorcycles, snow machines, jet skis and tractors. Cathy and he were best friends, confidants and competitive Parcheesi opponents. I enjoyed stepping into the role as his father and taking him on outdoor adventures.

Cathy was no stranger to hardship. She had lost her mother at age 9, her brother to a drunk driver when she was 19 and her father in 2006. Despite these tantamount losses, Cathy faced life courageously, living and breathing in each moment with a contagious air of peace about her. Little did we know there was greater loss to come.

Since age 19, Cathy had worked for the Fairbanks School District in the student records department. I was a heating contractor and began my business, Rocky's Heating Service. On the weekends, we focused on David and enjoyed the outdoors. And once in a while, we attended church.

I had gone to church most of my young life while growing up in Oklahoma. I had never been a big fan of church; the whole idea of God and religion seemed a bit stifling for a rugged, outdoorsy guy like me. I loved hunting, fishing, hiking, boating and joking around with the guys. Sitting in some boring church service when I

THE PATH BACK HOME

could be tearing up a dirt road or tossing my fishing line in the water didn't seem like much fun.

Cathy had first come to know God at 13. She was baptized shortly after — a way of publicly showing her church that she intended to follow the way of Jesus. But throughout high school, she fell off track and returned to partying. We both agreed it would be good to start attending church again once we married, but I still struggled to find its relevance in my life.

After David graduated high school, he moved to Washington and enrolled in the rigorous Construction Management Program at Washington State University. We were sad to see him go but excited for his new adventure. Cathy and I began attending services at Friends Church in Fairbanks; Cathy joined a Bible study and started reading the popular *Purpose-Driven Life* book by Pastor Rick Warren. I continued to take it all in from the sidelines, still convinced that truly giving my heart over to God would mean an end to my rough and tough manly ways.

༄༄༄

In May 2004, David called us from Seattle; he had graduated from the university the previous year and was working in Seattle. "Just calling to say hi. I'm on my way home from a party!" he announced.

"Are you on your motorcycle?" Cathy asked with a sigh. "Please, be careful on that thing, David."

LOVE STORY

"I will, Mom. I always am," David replied cheerfully. "Love you. I'll talk to you soon."

"Love you, too," Cathy replied, hanging up. She shook her head. "I really hope he's careful on that thing."

Early the next morning, the phone rang again. This time, it was a police officer's voice on the other end, somber as he said our names. "I'm afraid I have bad news. Your son, David, has been killed in a motorcycle accident."

There are no words to describe the way a parent feels when losing a child, no label to put on the moments between hearing those horrible, life-changing words and planning a funeral. Cathy and I waded through the following week in a daze, crying until it felt like the well inside our souls would dry up. We had lost our only son, the only child Cathy would ever have. It was devastating.

David's death was not just an incredible loss for us, but for the whole town. He was well loved by everyone; on an average day, his phone rang 200 times from friends all over the United States just calling to say hello. His goofy, loving spirit had touched many, prompting me to write "Fairbanks Lost a Son" when I penned his obituary.

David's friends gathered together at our home the week before the funeral and spent hours putting together a musical video tribute of our son. They stayed up all night, scanning photos into the computer, laughing and crying and reminiscing about the boy who impacted their lives.

We held David's funeral service at Friends Church. The outpouring of love and prayers from neighbors,

THE PATH BACK HOME

friends and church members was overwhelming. The sanctuary held 500, but it was so packed that people poured into the foyer.

As the 40-minute slideshow played, I glanced around and caught people laughing and crying as they remembered the tall broad-shouldered boy who brought so much life wherever he went. As I glanced back up at the front of the church, the coffin sitting on the steps jarred me out of the surreal setting. Tears streamed down my face as I tried to wrap my head around the fact that our once-vivacious son was lying in there. It was too painful to process.

During that dark time, something stirred inside of me. I had always believed in God, but suddenly I felt his presence, real, like never before. It was undeniable, as if he had reached his arms straight down from heaven and wrapped me in them. There seemed to be no other explanation for the peace and strength that got me out of bed each morning. I didn't know quite what this feeling was all about, but I knew I wanted more.

As Cathy and I grieved, we began attending Friends Church more regularly. I leaned forward in the service, hanging on every word the pastor said; his messages resonated with my heart.

"He makes being a Christian seem exciting," I told Cathy one day after church. "I always thought it was this legalistic thing, full of a bunch of rules, but I really believe there's more to it. Maybe there is room for a 40-ish outdoorsy guy like me in the church."

LOVE STORY

The hole in our lives where David had once been was glaring. We returned to work and continued attending Friends every week. In February 2005, I attended an evening class on the Holy Spirit. The pastor spoke about the intimate relationship we could have with God, and at last, the pieces finally clicked. God's Spirit was what had carried me through this dark time! It made such perfect sense. Christianity wasn't about a bunch of rules and regulations, but about a true and living relationship with God. *This* was what I wanted.

After the class ended, I bowed my head and prayed the prayer that would change the rest of my life. "Lord, I've known about you for a long time, but I truly want to know you now as my Savior. Please come into my heart. Forgive me of my wrongdoings, and please help me to follow you from this day forward."

As I drove home that night, praising God for the work in my heart, I realized something quite stunning: God had sent his only son, Jesus, to die on the cross for our sins. It had taken the death of my own son to point me back to Christ. My heavenly father and I had something in common.

Cathy and I threw ourselves into Bible study and other activities at church for the next few years. Cathy was growing in her own relationship with Christ; we were both excited to share our newfound faith.

☙☙☙

THE PATH BACK HOME

In early 2010, Cathy woke one morning feeling strange. "I'm weak all over," she complained. "I can barely move my arms."

I thought this was odd, but I wasn't too concerned. We continued with our day, but as the weeks passed, Cathy's symptoms grew worse. One evening, we sat down for pizza and began chatting. As we laughed, I noticed only one side of Cathy's face turned up in a smile. "Cathy!" I cried, alarmed. "What's going on with your face?"

Cathy looked at me with her big brown eyes, confused. My pizza stuck to my throat; I knew we had to get her to a doctor.

Through God's amazing provision, we got an appointment with world-renowned neurosurgeon Dr. Sekhar. Most people wait months to see this doctor, but we were able to land an appointment within the week. An MRI confirmed our concerns: Cathy had something wrong with her brain.

"A cavernoma, to be specific," Dr. Sekhar explained. "Basically, a massive blood leak, or hematoma, that is putting pressure on part of the brain and causing swelling. We need to go in and map out exactly where this hematoma is coming from and what parts of the brain it's affecting before we operate."

I swallowed hard. *Cavernoma* was a big word. So was *hematoma*. And *operation*? I squeezed Cathy's hand tightly and tried to take a deep breath. "It's going to be okay," I whispered. "God is in control." I reminded myself that we were in great hands, not only with Dr. Sekhar, but

LOVE STORY

with the creator of the universe. God would take care of my bride.

The doctors performed a battery of tests to map out the cavernoma before surgery. "They're going to put half of your brain to sleep," I explained to Cathy. "In other words," I added with a chuckle, "they're going to turn you into a man."

After reviewing the tests, Dr. Sekhar called us with the results. "I consulted with my neurosurgeon partner, and we have decided to access Cathy's cavernoma through the top of her head. This will greatly reduce the chances of affecting the other parts of the brain. We would also like to perform the surgery while she is asleep rather than awake as we originally thought, thus cutting down the operating time from eight or nine hours to five or six hours. We'll need to remove quite a large portion of the skull in surgery, so when we replace it, we'll secure it with small titanium plates."

Whoa. Lots of information. My brain was on overload, but I was confident in Dr. Sekhar's plan of action. I relayed the latest news to our good friends Jim and Misty Nordale. "So they're going to have her only use half her brain *and* make her hardheaded? They really *are* going to turn her into a man!" he joked.

It felt good to laugh in the midst of such serious circumstances. The Nordales insisted that I stay with them during Cathy's surgery and recovery, which would take place at Seattle Harborview Hospital.

I was grateful for their offer, as I had a hunch we'd be

THE PATH BACK HOME

away from home in Fairbanks for some time.

Just before we left Fairbanks, our friends Jeff and Gena Barney prayed with us. Jeff pulled out his Bible and read perhaps the most comforting words in the entire scriptures from Psalm 91: "Whoever dwells in the shelter of the Most High will rest in the shadow of the Almighty. I will say of the LORD, 'He is my refuge and my fortress, my God, in whom I trust.' Surely he will save you from the fowler's snare and from the deadly pestilence. He will cover you with his feathers, and under his wings you will find refuge; his faithfulness will be your shield and rampart."

I loved the image of God sheltering us with his wings, like a mama bird watching over her young. I trusted that God would take care of my bride and restore her health.

The night before the big day, 11-year-old Hanna Nordale handed Cathy a manila envelope. "Each kid in my class made you a card," she said with a shy smile. "Hope you like them."

Cathy smiled as she pulled each card from the envelope and read them with delight. One student had drawn two fish on a card and scrawled, "To Cathy Pavey, I hope your brain surgery goes swimmingly." We all chuckled, joking that Hanna's classmate might have a future at Hallmark.

The morning of the surgery, Cathy shared another Psalm that had spoken to her heart. "I woke up thinking of Psalm 23 this morning," she began. "The LORD is my shepherd, I lack nothing. He makes me lie down in green

LOVE STORY

pastures, he leads me beside quiet waters ..." (Psalm 23:1-2). As she quoted the rest of the passage, I realized it was the one we had had engraved on our son David's gravestone marker. How thankful we were to have the comfort in God's own words during this time.

Cathy and I arrived at Harborview Hospital at 6 a.m. on April 13, 2010. Her brother, Dave, and his wife, Toni, arrived a few minutes later. Dr. Sekhar came in to meet with us and said a prayer; I was immensely comforted by this. After he left, I pulled out my Bible and re-read Psalm 91. Friends and family had been writing and texting us with Bible verses the past few days, and I was so grateful once again for God's words.

"Rocky, please pray for God to comfort all of our friends and family who aren't here; I don't want them to be too worried about me," Cathy requested in her soft, sweet voice. I was amazed that just moments before a harrowing surgery, my wife thought not of herself but of our loved ones instead.

Around 7:15 a.m., the nurses came to wheel Cathy into the operating room on the gurney. I planted a big sloppy kiss on her mouth, and she returned the affection with a wide grin and a thumbs-up sign.

"If you get worried, just repeat these words: 'Thank you, Jesus; thank you, Jesus; thank you, Jesus,'" Cathy whispered, mustering a sweet smile. Even in her gown and cap, she looked beautiful, like an angel, not like a woman about to go have brain surgery.

I trudged into the waiting room and grabbed a cup of

THE PATH BACK HOME

bad hospital coffee to settle my nerves, musing that it didn't seem right to find a bad cup of coffee in Seattle.

My mind immediately turned to Cathy, my beautiful wife, and as the tears came, I gave them all to the Lord.

Seven long hours later, Dr. Sekhar called from the operating room. "The most critical portion of the surgery is over," he said. "We're in the process of sewing Cathy back up. To be honest, it was a very difficult surgery. We had to go in pretty deep because the cavernoma had grown so much. As of now, Cathy's motor skills seem to be intact, but we're not sure about her verbal skills just yet. We'll keep her sedated for another 24 hours to regulate her blood pressure and swelling."

The post-surgery ICU room was terribly dark and depressing; there were foreign-looking machines, with tubes and alarms that beeped intermittently. Nurses hustled about in the dim light like green-clad ghosts, whispering in hushed tones. I inched my way toward Cathy's bed and took a deep breath. She was still woozy from the anesthesia and hooked up to more machines and IVs than I'd ever seen in my life. Her chest rose and fell as she lay there, the same woman who just hours before had sweetly told me to pray if I got worried. Nothing could have prepared me for this difficult, dark moment. The nurses grew concerned when she was hardly able to respond to verbal and physical prompts.

"She's not coming around as we expected," the doctors said. "We're going to take her in for an MRI to make sure she hasn't had a stroke and isn't hemorrhaging."

LOVE STORY

Please, God, let her be okay. I collapsed onto the plastic hospital chair and played the waiting game once again. It was a horrible feeling to see my wife so helpless while I sat helpless as well, at the mercy of doctors and nurses. I reminded myself God was in control, that he held Cathy in his loving hands.

"Good news," the doctor reported when he came back into the room. "The MRI didn't show anything alarming; most likely she's just suffering the lasting effects of the anesthesia."

Over the next few hours, we all studied Cathy carefully. Occasionally, she wiggled her left hand or slightly opened her eyes. I grew anxious, just wishing she'd hop off the table, laugh and maybe even do the limbo for me. It was more difficult than I'd imagined to see my normally vivacious wife nearly lifeless on that bed, and for the first time since that morning, the tears flowed freely.

As the morning progressed, Cathy still could barely move her right side. "She may be having seizures, which is common after this type of surgery," a doctor explained. "The cavernoma was in a critical part of her brain that affects verbal skills, sleep motor skills and cognitive functions. It's not terribly surprising that she's having a difficult time coming around. Physical rehab is a high possibility in her future."

My head spun as I processed the information. It had just seemed so simple at first: go in and remove whatever was affecting Cathy's brain, and we could all get on with life.

THE PATH BACK HOME

Now it appeared we might have to walk down a very long, difficult road to recovery.

As Cathy continued to make minimal progress with her movement, the doctors reviewed the post-op MRIs with me. "There's a whitish color on the right hand control area on the MRI that is very concerning," Dr. Sekhar began. "This can often mean a stroke, but there is also a strong chance it's just severe swelling on the brain. Either one could cause the symptoms Cathy's having."

I returned to my laptop and updated my Caring Bridge Web site, which I'd been using to inform friends and family about Cathy's surgery. "Since God likes us to be specific in our prayers, please pray it's swelling and not a stroke," I wrote.

Cathy made minimal progress that day.

"Cathy, can you wiggle your fingers for us?" the doctors asked when they popped into the room to evaluate her.

Ever so slowly, Cathy lifted her right hand and tried to wiggle her fingers.

"Good job," the doctor said, smiling. "That's what we like to see!"

I stood to the side, encouraged. Never would I have thought such little movements would prove so exciting.

Thank you, God, I prayed. *My girl is in there. I just know she is.*

I slipped outside and headed to the small park area behind the hospital overlooking the harbor. As I sat down on a bench, the tears flowed, and my heart ached. I wanted

LOVE STORY

my Cathy back; this process was much more painful than I could have imagined. I was just entering into a really good pity-party when I noticed a woman striding toward me, a little Yorkshire Terrier on a leash beside her.

"Oh, you're an answer to prayers. I needed a little pick-me-up. Can I pet your dog?" I asked, wiping away my tears.

"Of course you can. Her name is Sugar." The woman stopped and smiled as I leaned down to pet her little dog.

"I have a Yorkie just like this back in Fairbanks," I told her. "My wife's beloved dog, actually. I can't wait to get back to her, but my wife's got to get better first."

"What's wrong with your wife?" she asked gently.

I told her about Cathy's surgery and that the recovery didn't seem to be going very well. "I'm very concerned for her long-term wellbeing," I admitted.

"I've had three brain surgeries. On the last one, they hit my verbal center, and I was in a coma for two weeks." She stepped back and waved her hands in front of her as if to say, "Look at me now!" Then she added, "My name is Nora, and I'll pray for you." She bent down and threw her arms around me in a long hug. "We serve a mighty God," she added with a smile as she pulled on her dog's leash. "Come on, Sugar," she called, and the two of them walked off.

New tears filled my eyes as she disappeared around the corner, tears of happiness this time. *Forgive me, Father, for my lack of faith. You have promised you would send your angels to hold us up so that we would not even strike*

THE PATH BACK HOME

our foot on a stone. You have said you would hear and rescue those who love you and who call upon your name. Thank you for sending this angel, Nora, to remind me of this promise.

Back in Cathy's hospital room, I sat beside her bed, squeezing her hand as I broke out into Merle Haggard tunes. My singing always made Cathy laugh, and I hoped that it might stir up at least a faint smile today, but instead she slept peacefully.

"I'm so proud of you, baby," I told her. "We all love you, and so many people are praying for you."

As I watched Cathy's chest rise and fall, it occurred to me that my relationship with God could often be like this. While I sat anxiously over Cathy, waiting for her to "show up," God did the same with me. He sat at my side, waiting patiently, saying, "Why, hello, child! I've been missing you!" when at last my eyelids fluttered open. In that moment, God comforted me once again, reminding me that he had planned this to happen from the very beginning of time and that he was weaving it all together for good, using his faithful servant Cathy to bring others to their knees.

Later that afternoon as I peeked in on Cathy, her eyes suddenly fluttered open. I raced to her side as she tilted her head and gave me a long, vacant stare.

My heart soared as I stared back into her big brown rounds.

"There you are! So good to see you!" I cried. I pulled up a chair and laid my hand on her bed. Slowly, she picked

LOVE STORY

up her hand, waved it around in a wobbly motion and then placed it firmly in mine and squeezed. I didn't move a muscle as I basked in the sweetness of the moment and her tender touch.

"I'm going to be here to hold your hand forever," I promised.

One huge tear appeared at the edge of her eye and rolled down her cheek. "Oh, Lord, she's in there!" My heart sang with joy.

My friend Dave Whitmer flew in that night to be with me. He and I sang renditions of "Amazing Grace" to Cathy and lulled her to sleep with our off-key music. A few minutes later, as I typed away at my laptop, Dave nudged me.

"Look at Cathy!" he cried.

Cathy's right hand, which had been resting on her stomach, now slowly climbed up her chest toward her neck. "I do believe she's trying to cover her ears because of our singing," I laughed. "Boy, am I insulted." Cathy's movements may have been slow, but her surgery certainly hadn't affected her eardrums!

Mornings proved to be hardest at the hospital. Cathy lay quiet and unresponsive, the halls were dark and quiet and I was growing tired of the stale hospital coffee. Mornings were when the devil seemed to taunt me with his old tricks and tried to discourage me.

One of the ICU doctors discussed Cathy's progress in frank detail. "In truth, we don't know what the future

THE PATH BACK HOME

holds for Cathy," he said. "She most likely has a long road of recovery ahead."

Downtrodden, I trudged out back to the little park I had come to know as my Garden of Sorrow. There, Satan stepped up his game, haunting me with thoughts like, *Give up, it's useless. This whole thing is all your fault.*

But in that moment, God spoke to me, reminding me of his truth. I poured out my heart to him, telling him my fears and struggles. *Trust me. I am the Great Physician,* I heard him say.

Thirty minutes later, my wife's dear friend Linda Sather sent me an e-mail that pierced my heart to the core. She shared how she had gone through major brain surgery five years before and wrote in great detail about her journey to recovery. After hearing one doctor after another say, "We don't know exactly what will happen with Cathy; everyone's recovery is different," it was so comforting to read about Linda's journey and feel in my heart that Cathy was going to be okay. Linda's words were exactly what I needed at that very moment.

God's timing: impeccable.

❧❧❧

One morning, 11 days after surgery, I got a brilliant idea. I grabbed a bottle of lotion and began massaging Cathy's feet. As I moved from her left foot to the right, I said, "Cathy, if you want me to continue, you're going to have to pick up your foot." Ever so slowly, she lifted her

LOVE STORY

little toes off the bed. Dave and I stared at her, wide-eyed with excitement. Movement from the right side meant her delayed progress was due to swelling in the brain, not a stroke. This was great news!

Dr. Sekhar confirmed this when he asked her to move her right toes and her leg. "Yup, it's swelling. She'll get better. It's just going to take a long time."

Later that day, Cathy's brother and his wife announced it was time for them to head back to Fairbanks. Toni leaned forward and kissed Cathy's forehead. "We're so proud of you," she whispered. "We will be back as soon as we can." Cathy's eyes filled with tears, and so did ours. My girl was still in there, fighting for her life.

Cathy's slow progress continued. One morning, the nurses entered to find Cathy had pulled her feeding tube out during the night. "Look at you, making trouble again," the nurse teased as she proceeded to reinsert the tube.

Suddenly, Cathy rose up from her pillow and blurted out a string of curse words. "&*$*!" she cried out, her voice strong and confident as could be.

We all stared at her in disbelief for a moment, then burst out laughing. "Well, what do you know! My baby is back and cursing like a sailor!" I laughed.

Cathy just sat there with a coy smile, as if to say, "What? What's so funny?"

I laughed again. These weren't the particular words I would have chosen for her comeback debut, but we were so happy to hear her speak, it hardly mattered what she said.

THE PATH BACK HOME

I sat down and took Cathy's hands. "I'm so proud of you!" I gushed. "We all love you so much. You're doing so well." Cathy looked like she had so much to say, but no more words escaped her mouth. Instead, we sat there, holding hands like two giddy high schoolers on a first date.

One evening, Cathy opened her mouth and began talking in a small, nearly inaudible voice. I knelt before her and said shakily, "Cathy, tell me what my name is."

She reached her wobbly left arm up, cupped the back of my head and whispered distinctly, "Turd."

"No, honey, tell me my real name. The name you use in public!" Inside, I was dying of laughter. Turd was the name Cathy had affectionately dubbed me at home. It appeared my girl's memory was indeed returning.

That night, as I sifted through the many e-mails our friends and family had sent, one in particular caught my eye. "Rocky, I read about your wife, Cathy. I'm so sorry to hear about her situation. I haven't prayed much in the past 20 years, but I'm going to start praying right now." Again, God reminded me that he was working all things together for good, weaving together a beautiful tapestry that he would one day reveal. *The fabric is the body of Christ, and I am using Cathy, my dear child, as the needle,* he said.

Cathy's progress: three steps forward, two steps backward the next few days. When Dr. Sekhar asked her where she was, she promptly said, "Seattle." She even used the words "Rocky" and "handsome" in the same sentence,

LOVE STORY

which we all found baffling and amusing. But the next few days, her confusion returned, and I grew concerned. Was she experiencing seizures?

I decided to lighten things up with my famous singing again. I tried lulling Cathy to sleep with Merle Haggard tunes, and within no time, her eyelids grew heavy, and she drifted off to sleep.

As Cathy rested, I slipped out back to my Garden of Sorrow, which I'd recently renamed the Park of Praise. I sat down, lit a cigar and thanked God for Cathy's healing progress. My dear friend Jim Nordale had specially ordered my favorite cigars for me, and I was grateful for his kind gesture. As I prayed, I grew distracted and accidentally put the lit side of the cigar in my mouth.

"Ouch!" I yelped, jumping up as the hot cigar burnt my tongue. Reeling from the burn, I fumbled with the cigar and quickly wrapped up my prayer. I chuckled at myself as I strode back inside. Once again, God lifted my spirits with light moments like these.

൳൳൳

Almost two weeks after the surgery, Cathy progressed from a feeding tube to gooey foods like applesauce, yogurt, cranberry juice, milk and ice cream. I snuck the leftover ice cream sometimes, considering it a favor for Cathy and the doctors as I kept her blood sugar down.

In the evenings, when Cathy was more coherent, I tried joking around with her. Cathy continued to speak in

THE PATH BACK HOME

a nearly inaudible voice, but it was often difficult to discern when she was making a joke because of her "flat face." As the doctors explained, Cathy's face muscles had not yet re-learned to express themselves, so she did not smile, raise her eyebrows, purse her lips or wrinkle her nose like one normally would. This made our conversations hilarious and a bit unnerving at the same time.

Two weeks after we entered that hospital, I wheeled Cathy outside into the Seattle sunshine for the first time. The Nordales had brought their new German wire-haired pointer puppy, Ellie, upon Cathy's request. We helped Cathy out of her wheelchair, set her on a blanket and let Ellie climb up onto her lap. Slowly, Cathy stroked her, an unsure smile slowly creeping onto her face. She seemed rather frightened of the dog, but we praised the Lord for that smile anyhow.

As we sat there, basking in the sunshine, Nora, my angel, and her dog, Sugar, walked up. "What a coincidence!" she said to Cathy. "I've been praying so hard for you, girl." In that moment, we all knew it was not a coincidence, but a divine appointment by God himself. What a wonderful day!

With some convincing from our dear friend Kathy Hughes, Cathy's therapists recommended her for the intensive live-in rehab facility on the fourth floor. This was a big deal, as there were only so many available beds for patients on this floor. We praised God for this "golden ticket" opportunity; Harborview was known for its

LOVE STORY

outstanding rehab facility, and we felt much more comfortable having Cathy there than moving her to an outpatient facility.

Late one Monday night, as I typed another entry into the Caring Bridge site, God spoke to me about the difference between hope and faith. "Hope is born of fear and worry. Faith is born of trust."

I said two sentences out loud: "I *hope* she'll get better." There was worry in that. I tried it again: "I have *faith* she will get better." One sentence came from desperation, the other from confidence in Christ. In the moments when Cathy seemed to regress, my panic quickly returned, and I succumbed to worry. I had to live in faith, constantly seeking the Lord and trusting him.

"Oh, Lord, forgive my weaknesses," I prayed through tears that night. "Heal me, as you've healed my wife. I need your strength."

୰୰୰

On Thursday, April 29th, Cathy left the third-floor neuro care wing and moved on up to the fourth-floor rehab center. I shared the good news with Cathy's brother, who flew in that day. "It must be all the prayers from everyone," I said excitedly. "You should see all the hits the Web site has gotten. More than 10,000 to date! It looks like Cathy's gone viral!"

At that moment, a nurse walked in and happened to hear the last part of my sentence. She went into "Code

THE PATH BACK HOME

Red" mode and started poking Cathy with needles to pump her with antibiotics and IV fluids.

"I think there's been a misunderstanding," I tried to explain. "By viral, I meant …" I glanced over at Dave, and we cracked up.

Though Cathy still struggled with movement on her right side and often remained confused, talking about herself in third person, her sense of humor began to return. One day, after I returned from the store with some fresh fruit for her, she cocked her head back, stared at me and said, "And who are you?"

I began to shake, panic stricken at the thought that she might have had a hemorrhage or stroke. Just as I was about to lose it, Cathy gave a little snort and grinned. "I know who you are, Turd," she said. I had always been the jokester in our relationship, but now it seemed the doctors had activated the "funny" center in my wife's brain when they went in. I was going to have some serious future competition!

It felt so good to laugh again. God had put joy where there was once fear, peace where there was once worry, faith where there was once a shaky hope. Cathy and I exchanged jokes back and forth; thankfully, she seemed to have forgotten all my old ones, and I could recycle them again. As they say, laughter is truly the best medicine of all.

As Cathy settled into her new private room on the rehab floor, Dr. Sekhar came to me with her latest MRI results.

LOVE STORY

"There's a small triangle-shaped piece of white material on the outer edge of the image, probably a tiny piece of the cavernoma left behind in surgery. At this point, it's nothing to be concerned about," he explained. "The good news is that everything else looks great."

I praised God once again for good news.

As I did, he reminded me of a wonderful Bible verse, 1 Corinthians 13:12: "Now we see things imperfectly as in a cloudy mirror, but then we will see everything with perfect clarity..."

Some days, the picture was still fuzzy, much like Cathy's memory. But in the end, I believed God was working all things for good, still weaving that magnificent tapestry that he would someday unveil for all to see.

On May 1st, I witnessed one of the greatest acts of kindness in human history. Tom Bartels, proprietor of North Pole's Coffee Roasters, sent me a care package with two pounds of "Black Gold" blend coffee. Real, authentic, delicious non-hospital coffee. For a guy who had spent the past few weeks drinking questionable, murky decaf coffee, this was simply a dream come true. It also worked wonders when bribing the nurses for a little extra attention for my beautiful bride.

On May 2nd, I witnessed yet another exciting event. Cathy asked to type something on the computer. It took her two whole hours, but she managed to eke out a few precious lines:

THE PATH BACK HOME

Hi, everyone, Big Rocky and my brother, Dave, are here keeping this thing going! Thank you, thank you for letting me ride along. Go, me, go. Fight, fight, fight! Cathy.

Encouraging responses poured in left and right, proof that Cathy's fan club was growing by the day.

That evening, we celebrated our wedding anniversary together. The Nordales picked up King Crab with all the trimmings from our favorite place, The Fisherman's Restaurant, as well as tiramisu and blueberry cheesecake from the Cheesecake Factory. They also brought a few extras to complete the romantic setting: white linens, real silver candleholders and two long dinner candles.

"This is absolutely perfect, isn't it?" I said to Cathy, serving her a bite of delicious crab. The nurses stopped by and seemed alarmed by the candles, commenting that the place might catch on fire. I reminded them that the hospital had an excellent burn unit should things go bad.

After dinner, I wrapped Cathy in a new quilt and walked her out to the park. We sat there for more than an hour, watching the sun descend and the lights flicker in the skyscrapers.

"I think this may just be the best anniversary we ever had," I told Cathy, squeezing her hand.

Back in the room, we admired the 25 beautiful handmade paper butterflies Emmi Nordale's class had made for Cathy. As we taped them up on the wall, I read each encouraging message to her. "Dear Cathy, we are

LOVE STORY

praying for you. We hope these butterflies help you feel better." In no time at all, those drab hospital walls were cheery and bright.

❧❧❧

Cathy grew stronger the next few days; each feat was exciting, like watching a child take steps for the first time. She insisted on showering herself, curling and blow-drying her hair and putting on makeup. I resisted the urge to help her curl her hair and cringed when her weak right hand slipped and the hot curling iron touched her forehead. At last, I could stand it no longer and took over curling iron duties. This amused both Cathy, myself and Cathy's brother, Dave, who happened to walk in just as I perfected her bangs.

The doctors were amazed by Cathy's progress. Each time a new doctor walked onto the rehab floor, the other doctors brought him in and introduced him to Cathy. "This is the person we've been telling you about," the old docs said as Cathy beamed back. Once again, I knew the credit belonged only to God, the Great Physician, and, of course, to the many prayers from around the country and beyond.

Cathy continued working with the physical therapist every day, taking small walks and working on regaining her strength.

Her speech and memory remained a challenge; she had a communication disorder called aphasia that made it

THE PATH BACK HOME

difficult for her to start a conversation. "This is not something we can cure," the doctors said. "She just may never be as talkative as she once was." I bit my tongue to keep from joking, "And this is a bad thing *because?*"

The speech therapist encouraged Cathy to write in a journal to regain control over her fine motor skills and to work her memory muscles. The occupational therapist came, too, and helped Cathy with simple chores, like doing laundry. It hit me that she was re-learning everything again, like a child venturing off on her own for the first time. We still had a long road ahead, but Cathy was making remarkable strides.

Mother's Day rolled around, and the Nordales showed up at the hospital park with a trunk load of food for what they announced was the "First and Last Annual Harborview Get Well/Mother's Day Picnic." We enjoyed a spectacular day on the lawn; the weather was a perfect 70 degrees, the potato salad was delicious and the company was even better. It was a bittersweet day, however, as we remembered our dear son, David Alan. His brilliant smile and sweet, goofy spirit remained forever etched in our hearts, and we did not try to ignore the pain in our hearts on this Mother's Day. They say sorrow shared is halved and joy shared is doubled, and as we sprawled on that hospital lawn with our dear friends and watched the sun go down, we realized we'd had a little of both that day.

One night, Cathy and I sat together enjoying deli sandwiches with Toni, sent from our friends the Manzies.

LOVE STORY

"Who wants a little dinner music?" I asked.

Toni raised an eyebrow. "So long as you aren't providing it," she said with a laugh.

I borrowed a friend's iPod, and the beautiful Kutless song "Word of God Speak" wafted through the room. Halfway through the song, I glanced over and saw Cathy with her palms turned upward toward heaven, tears streaming down her face, singing along with the words. "I am so thankful," she whispered.

Later that night, Cathy told me, "When David died, I was so ready to go home and be with him. But God told me he wasn't through with me yet."

"That's right. He wasn't through with you yet," I agreed. God was still weaving that beautiful tapestry with a needle tempered with the fire of trials and faith. Someday, his majestic work will be revealed to our eyes.

ے۔ے۔ے۔

On May 11th, exactly four weeks after surgery, Cathy was released from the hospital. She still had a ways to go with her recovery, but we planned to resume rehabilitation with therapists back in Fairbanks when we got home. To celebrate, the Nordales cooked a New York steak, which Cathy devoured in no time. It took nearly five hours to pack up all her cards, gifts, pictures and personal items people had showered her with.

As we walked out toward the park that afternoon, an ICU nurse I recognized walked toward us. She introduced

THE PATH BACK HOME

herself as Megan and seemed very excited to see Cathy walking and talking. "Normally, patients in your condition are in rehab for months and months. We never get to see their end results," she gushed. "You look great!"

Once again, I praised God as the realization that my wife could have been bedridden and incoherent for months hit me like a speeding train. My wife was a walking miracle, a testimony to God's amazing faithfulness and healing hand. And a testimony, of course, to the power of prayer.

Cathy celebrated her "great escape" with a plate of our friend Susan Sele's famous brownies and a trip to the hairstylist for a much-needed color and trim. She walked out of that salon a redhead, and I had to do a double take from the little coffee shop table where I sat. It would take some getting used to, but I was pretty sure the redhead thing would grow on me.

We returned home to a front yard full of balloons, yellow ribbons, posters, signs and lawn angels, all placed by friends, family and neighbors. The inside of the house was filled with goodies, posters, ice cream and a fridge full of delectable dinners. "Looks like just a couple people love you," I said with a wink, pulling my beautiful bride in for a hug. "Did I happen to tell you that I'm one of them?"

"Are you going to start singing Merle Haggard right now?" Cathy asked, laughing.

"Only if you do the limbo," I replied with a grin.

☙☙☙

LOVE STORY

So that was the middle of our story. There was much more, of course, but you get the gist. God worked a miracle in our lives, replacing the losses and hardships with miracles, provision and healing. Today, a year and a half after her surgery, Cathy and I live a simple but happy life, and I am pleased to say I am more in love with my wife than I've ever been before. We enjoy long walks with the dogs, gardening and being outdoors when the finicky Alaska weather permits. I belong to a group called Wild-Hearted Alaska Men (WHAM), comprised of outdoorsy guys like myself who love the Lord and enjoy fishing, hunting, canoeing, snowmobiling and hiking. I purchased an airplane as well and am in the process of obtaining my pilot's license, which I think concerns Cathy just a tad. She may stay on the ground and wave.

Three months after surgery, her occupational and speech therapist met with her boss and co-workers to determine what they could do to get her ready for work again. But those she worked with wanted her to come back right away and said they'd help her. The job would be her therapy. Her boss, Janet, tailored Cathy's duties to her abilities and assigned someone to work right alongside her to help her remember things.

This was — and is — a huge blessing to Cathy and me. They are understanding if she needs to leave for a two-hour lunch break to take a nap. And several of the ladies Cathy works with started having prayer meetings for her when she was in the hospital, and some have come to visit Friends Community Church at different times.

THE PATH BACK HOME

"Cool!" one friend said one day when she walked into the sanctuary, greeted by so many genuine smiling faces.

We have received a continuous outpouring of support for Cathy at Friends Church. At last, I've found a place I can be transparent with other men who love the Lord and love to have fun. We feel so blessed to call this place our home.

This side of heaven, I may never know how many lives were impacted by Cathy's journey. I do know this, though: We serve a great and mighty God, and just as he promised in Psalm 91, he watched over my wife and brought healing and hope to our lives.

≈≈≈

"How was your day?" I asked Cathy when she came home from work one evening. Her eyes looked weary, and I sensed she'd had enough activity for one day. As much as Cathy loved her job, her "new" self wore out a bit more easily than the old one.

"I'm tired. I think I'm going to … go to the place … where I sleep," Cathy replied sleepily.

"Going to bed?" I asked, smiling. Cathy still sometimes fumbled for the right word when speaking.

"Yes, bed." Cathy laughed. "I love you, Rocky."

"I love you, too." I planted a kiss on her forehead and helped her down the hall to our room.

This may be no castle, and I may be no king, but I certainly feel like I've found that princess in my own

LOVE STORY

fairytale, I thought to myself as I tucked my bride into bed with one last goodnight kiss.

… And they lived happily ever after? I like to think so.

AVAILABLE
The Story of Vance Lindstrom
Written by Karen Koczwara

The car came to a screeching halt as it hit the tree with a deafening thud. I braced my legs against the dashboard and covered my eyes just in time. When I dared to open them, I saw my grandmother lying limp on the seat, blood dripping from her nose, her eyes closed. I had never seen a dead person, but in my gut, I knew the truth. She was gone.

My heart raced, adrenaline pumping through my veins as I scrambled to push open the passenger door. In the backseat, my brother and sister whimpered softly. I had to get us help and fast! Every minute counted. Why wouldn't this stubborn door open?

At last, I gave up on the door and slid through the half-open car window, my legs shaking as I landed on my feet. One glance at the front of the car, and I knew I was lucky to be alive. The entire front engine of the little Subaru was wrapped around a thick tree; it was too horrific to think about. *Help, help, help.* The words pounded in my brain before they echoed from my mouth. "Help!" I cried, sliding on the gravel as I raced toward the road.

Just feet away, my brother and sister continued to cry, their frightened sobs growing louder, drowning out my pounding heart. Things like this only happened in scary movies, not to a couple of small-town kids out for a

THE PATH BACK HOME

leisurely drive. *Please, someone help.* I had never felt more alone.

As a truck rounded the bend, I felt my knees go weak. I jumped up and down and waved my arms frantically as the vehicle slowed. Relief washed over me, but just as quickly, I remembered, and my heart sank to the ground. My beloved grandmother was dead.

☙☙☙

Elgin, Oregon, is the sort of town one might pass through on a leisurely drive through the scenic Blue Mountains on a summer afternoon. Nestled between sprawling pine trees and picturesque green meadows, this little logging town in Eastern Oregon is a hunter's paradise. But young boys sometimes grow restless in small towns, and it didn't take long for trouble to find its way to my front door.

I was born on April 21, 1970. My parents met in the tiny town of Halfway, Oregon, at a party for the Apollo moon landing. Not long after that wild night, my mother discovered she was pregnant; she was just a high school senior. She gave birth to me in Baker, Oregon, and soon told my father about his new son. My father stepped up and married my mother in September 1971. My younger sister, Kathy, came along in July 1972, and my brother, Craig, followed a year later.

Eventually we moved into a doublewide trailer on a sprawling corner lot in Elgin. My brother and I bunked

AVAILABLE

together, while my sister took the room next to ours. A sturdy pine tree sat just outside our window, and out back, we planted a large vegetable garden. My mother stayed home with us during the day and often worked nights as a cook and a bartender at local restaurants. My father was a log truck driver. We were, for the most part, your average small-town American family.

"Vance! Get inside! It's way past your bedtime!" my mother called, pushing open the creaky back screen door. "And wipe that dirt off you before you come in!"

"All right, comin'!" I hollered back, dropping my plastic army men in the dirt and trudging through the garden toward the house. I wiped my feet and brushed past my mother, but not fast enough to escape her inspection.

"Honestly, Vance! How one boy gets so dirty so quickly is beyond me!" She laughed, though, her brown eyes sparkling as she smoothed her work apron over her slender hips. I loved my mother's enthusiasm for life; she was always laughing, always the first one to run to her friends with a juicy piece of gossip. My father, with his dark hair and clean-shaven smile, was a bit more subdued, always taking life in quietly. Compared to the two of them, I was very shy.

When I started elementary school, my parents decided to send us to church. Though they didn't attend church themselves, the relatives on my father's side did, and my parents thought it would be a good idea for us to go, too. "Better get ready for church," my mother said one Sunday

THE PATH BACK HOME

morning, glancing up as she sipped her morning coffee. "Do you want me to drive you?"

"No. We can walk," I answered as I turned to go pick out my least wrinkled shirt and a pair of slacks. I liked going to church. The songs were fun, the stories were pretty interesting and sometimes, if we were lucky, we got a little snack, too.

During the summer, we attended Vacation Bible School. This was like a weeklong day camp filled with more stories, songs, snacks and even games. I listened intently as the leaders shared about a God who loved us and read us stories from the Bible. My aunt Kay often talked about this God who loved us, too, and I wondered why I didn't hear more about him at home.

One afternoon in the fifth grade, I picked up a crossword puzzle book sitting on my parents' coffee table. As I thumbed through, my eyes fell onto an advertisement in the middle of the book. "Do you want to experience money, fame and power?" it read. My eyes grew wide as I scanned the page. It went on to say that through witchcraft, one could find everything he'd ever dreamed of. I was immediately intrigued.

"Check this out," I whispered to my brother and sister that night, whipping the book out of my pocket. "This says we can have money, fame and power if we just send away for this stuff! Maybe we could make some extra money weeding the garden to pay for it. What do you think?"

"I dunno, sounds kinda weird," my sister replied, looking unimpressed.

AVAILABLE

"Come on! Don't you want to be rich and famous like those kids on TV?" I insisted. But even as I said the words, something inside me grew uneasy. I thought about my time at Vacation Bible School: *What would God think of this?*

When they left the room, I re-read the words on the page. At the end, to my surprise, it read, "And God doesn't mind." I sucked in my breath. So there I had it! God didn't mind if I sent away for this. Why, he probably *wanted* me to be rich and famous. All my dreams were going to come true. This small-town boy was going to strike it rich!

The next Sunday morning, I re-read the article to my brother and sister before we left for Sunday school. This time, I read them the line that I had just discovered: "God doesn't mind." Since we were all now convinced that it was okay, we began to plan how to raise the money to buy the book.

Arriving at the church, we each went to our separate classes. As I settled into my seat in the classroom, the Sunday school teacher strode into the classroom with an unusually solemn look on her face. "Good morning, class," she began, glancing around the room nervously. "I, uh, I have no idea why I need to talk about this this morning, but I strongly feel that I'm supposed to share about witchcraft and why it is wrong."

I sat glued to my seat, stunned by her words. Immediately, I thought of the crossword puzzle book.

"Witchcraft can seem very harmless, but it is actually of the devil, and it's very dangerous," my teacher

THE PATH BACK HOME

continued. As she continued to speak, my uneasiness grew; she seemed to be talking directly to me.

After church, I shared her words with my brother and sister. "You'll never believe what my teacher talked about today," I blurted. "She talked about witchcraft!"

When I got home, I raced to my room and picked up the magazine again. When my eyes fell onto the advertisement, I was shocked to see that the words "And God won't mind" were nowhere to be found. I searched the page over and over, but they were gone. Had I imagined it? Were my eyes playing tricks on me? No, I knew that I had read it several times. I even knew where it was on the page. But now it was gone. What was going on here?

When I was in the sixth grade, my life was changed forever one sunny afternoon. My grandmother drove me, my brother and sister home from a visit to our Christian relatives in Washington State; I chattered happily in the front seat as her little Subaru wound through the tree-dotted two-lane road. Six miles outside Elgin, my grandmother suddenly veered off the road, and the car barreled straight toward a large tree. Instinctively, I braced my legs against the dashboard just as the car hit the tree with a resounding thud. The horrible sound of crunching metal echoed in my ears as the car jolted to a stop and I bounced out of my seat.

The next few minutes were a blur of confusion and panic. I glanced over at my grandmother; blood spurted from her nose, and she was not moving. Frantic, I glanced

AVAILABLE

over at my brother and sister, who were both crying hysterically in the backseat. "Help!" I cried, my heart thudding wildly in my chest. I tried to open the passenger door, but it was jammed. Hastily, I climbed out of the half-open window instead. My legs wobbled as I jumped onto the gravel road below.

Don't let Grandma be dead, my mind repeated over and over as I willed my legs to propel me to the edge of the road. A work truck came around the bend; I jumped up and down and waved my arms frantically. "Stop! Please help!"

The truck pulled over, and two men jumped out. "You okay, son? What happened?" one asked, running toward the scene.

I could hardly get the words out. "My grandmother … my brother and sister … we hit that tree … unconscious!" I fought to find my breath as the men surveyed the wreckage behind us.

One of the men grabbed a first aid kit and raced toward the car to help my brother and sister. The other got on the radio and called for the local ambulance. Within minutes, I heard sirens in the background; help was on the way.

"I'm afraid she's dead," the paramedic announced after searching for my grandmother's pulse. "Let's get you kids to the clinic."

This was all happening too quickly. I pulled my legs under my chin as the ambulance sped down the road. I had imagined what the insides of ambulances looked like

THE PATH BACK HOME

many times, picturing the many contraptions, wires, lights and the gurney, but this wasn't how I wanted to find out. My beloved grandmother was dead. Just like that, she'd vanished from my life forever. There would be no more memories, no bedtime stories, no laughs over the kitchen table. She was simply gone.

My mother was waiting for us at the local clinic; she raced toward us in tears. "Oh, Lord! What happened? The neighbor called and said you were in an accident …" Her voice trailed off as she hugged me fiercely. "Thank God you're okay!"

"Grandma's dead," I managed to say, still in shock.

My brother, sister and I escaped the accident with only minor injuries, but there was a gaping hole in our lives after my grandmother passed away. The trauma of that day led my mother to become an Emergency Medical Technician with Elgin's ambulance crew. One day, my mother shared something amazing. "The ambulance responded to an accident today. Apparently, the first people to arrive were the same two men who stopped for your accident. The EMTs said that those two guys have been the first ones to arrive at many other accidents around town over the years. They always show up with the right equipment and the right skills for the situation … and as soon as the ambulance shows up and has everything under control, they just suddenly disappear. The whole ambulance crew thinks that they must be angels. There were angels watching over you, son."

I sucked in my breath. Was it possible that they'd

AVAILABLE

really been angels? The thought was both comforting and puzzling. I'd heard my Sunday school teacher talk about angels in church, but I'd always pictured them with wings and a halo, floating around up in heaven and singing hymns with a harp, not two rugged men in an old work truck.

As I entered junior high, I slowly drifted away from church and sought out a new crowd of friends. My best friend, Tom, whom I'd grown up with, approached me one evening as I spent the night at his house. "Hey, Vance, my parents have a bunch of liquor in the cupboard. No one's around, so what do you say we sneak some," he whispered.

I snickered. "Won't they notice?"

"Nah. There's so much of it stashed up there, I doubt they'll ever notice," he assured me.

"All right," I replied. I was curious. My dad always drank beer after work, and I had sampled it when no one was looking, but I had never tasted hard alcohol before.

We snuck into the kitchen and pulled a couple bottles out of the cabinet. "You go first," I insisted, watching as my friend untwisted the cap on a bottle of rum.

Tom smiled, tilted his chin back and took a long swig of the stuff. "Whoa, strong!" He shuddered and then laughed as he handed the bottle to me. "Your turn, man."

I took a small sip of the liquor and then a longer one. It left a bitter taste in my mouth, but I liked how relaxed I felt within minutes. "Hmm, think we could do this again sometime?" I asked with a smile.

THE PATH BACK HOME

"Sure. Like I said, they'll never notice."

Tom and I made many more stops to that liquor cabinet in junior high. Eventually we noticed that the bottles were getting empty, and we needed to stop to avoid getting caught. By now we were getting hooked. It was then that Tom came upon a brilliant idea. His mom had a bottle of rum extract in the cupboard. By adding water to the rum extract, we would make rum. "Cheap way to get drunk, huh?" he said with a sly smile as he stirred the extract into a glass. "They don't teach this stuff in home economics."

I laughed. "Nope, they sure don't." We both gulped down our rum mix — and to this day, I still cannot stand the taste of butter rum Lifesavers!

I continued drinking throughout high school. Mostly, we snuck beers from our parents. Eventually, though, it was my turn to have a brilliant idea. I discovered that wine was made by mixing fruit juice and a special yeast. So, I proposed that we make our own alcohol by mixing sugar water and bread yeast. After letting it ferment in Tom's closet for a few weeks, we decided to try it. Tom was the first to try it, since it had been in his closet. He took a gulp, then began coughing and choking. In response, I decided not to try it. The memory of our "rum" invention was still fresh in my mind.

In time, we found a steady source of alcohol for our parties. My friend Scott's mother was divorced and had a series of boyfriends. In an effort to gain Scott's approval, they would often buy him cases of beer. When the

AVAILABLE

weekend rolled around, my friends and I piled into our cars and headed out to the old dirt road just outside of town to drink. I desperately wanted to remain a cool kid, and everyone knew partying was the best way to stay cool in high school.

"Hey, Scott, good to see you, man!" I called out as he jumped out of his car with a 12-pack of beer. "See you brought the beer. Nice!"

"Can always count on me," Scott replied breezily. He ripped open the pack and popped the top on a beer can before passing the rest around. And there, beneath the stars on that old dirt road, I got drunk and laughed until my sides hurt as much as my head. It was just another Friday night.

One weekend, I joined Tom on a trip to his grandparents' place in Halfway. As I packed my things, my father strode into my room. "So, Vance, is there going to be beer where you're going?" he asked, staring at me sternly.

I knew that someone in Halfway had already offered to buy us a couple cases of beer for a party, but I didn't want to give my father reason to not let me go. "Maybe a little," I replied coolly.

"Well, I'll let you go, but I don't want you getting drunk, you hear me?" His eyes met mine, pleading as if to say, "Can I trust you, son?"

"I promise, Dad, I won't," I insisted, grabbing my things. "Now, I gotta get going. Tom's gonna be here any minute."

THE PATH BACK HOME

As the little town of Halfway came into view, Tom nudged me.

"You ready to have some fun?" he asked, grinning.

"I'm more than ready," I replied, smiling back. I gazed out at the sprawling green fields where hundreds of cows roamed. The joke around Halfway was that there were more cows than people. It was here that my mother and father had first met at a wild party themselves. I knew my father's family had a history of alcoholism, which explained his concern for my drinking. I respected him, but at the same time, life was short, and I just wanted to have a little fun like everyone else.

Not long after we arrived at Tom's grandparents', we ran to the local store to buy our beer. And not long after that, we all got drunk. When I returned home, my father cornered me again. "You got drunk, didn't you?" he pressed.

"Not really," I replied, trying to avoid eye contact as I unpacked my things.

"Vance, look me in the eye, and tell me you didn't get drunk," my father said, raising his voice just a notch.

I stared at the floor, feeling his eyes bore into the back of my head. At last, I raised my eyes to meet his. "I got drunk, okay?" I admitted.

"Vance, you promised not to get drunk. And then you went out and did it, anyway. Do you want to end up an alcoholic? Is that what you want? You better get your head together, and stop messing around. Do you understand me?" He stormed out of the room.

AVAILABLE

My father was generally a loving and patient man; rarely had I seen him get so angry. As I climbed into bed, I thought long and hard about what I was doing. I didn't want to hurt my parents, for they were good people. But I wasn't ready to give up my fun, my good times with the popular crowd, just yet.

The next morning, my mother's disappointed eyes met mine. "Your father told me," she said quietly, plunking my breakfast down on the table. I expected her to say more, but her silence spoke volumes.

I didn't have any words myself. I knew I'd let them down, but I couldn't promise I wouldn't do it again. Instead, I dove into my eggs in silence. Alcohol was driving a wedge between me and my family. As a result, I began to drink even more.

My junior year of high school, Tom invited me to a party at his house. "We're going to play 'quarters,' and you're gonna go first," he announced when I arrived, tossing a beer can my way.

"Oh, yeah?" I glanced around the room and was surprised to see how many of my peers had showed up. It was going to be a full house tonight, and I was happy to be right in the middle of the action.

We each took turns trying to bounce a quarter into a glass of beer. Whenever someone was successful, we would race one another to drink a can of beer. The slowest drinker had to drink the beer from the glass. As the night progressed, I downed one drink after another, until my head pounded and the room began to spin. I was used to

THE PATH BACK HOME

binge drinking, but tonight I was drinking even more than usual. *Plink!* Another quarter landed in the glass, and everyone began to gulp down another beer. My stomach began to churn, and just as I finished the last drop of my beer, the entire contents of my insides flew onto the table.

I laid my spinning head down on the table, covering my forehead with beer and vomit. Behind me, I heard snickers, then full-blown laughter. Embarrassed, I began to laugh with them.

"Nice one, Vance!" a guy called out, slapping my back as he cackled.

"Oh, man, there goes breakfast, lunch and dinner!" another chimed in, laughing as he stepped away from the mess.

"I'll clean it up, don't worry," I stammered, suddenly mortified by the scene I'd caused. I stumbled into Tom's bathroom and grabbed a wad of paper towels. As I glanced into the mirror, I hardly recognized myself with the bloodshot eyes, rumpled hair and drool running down my mouth. Who had I become?

That Monday at school, several of my peers stopped to harass me about my little incident. "Heard you puked your guts out Saturday night," one guy said, snickering as he passed me in the hall. "Way to impress the ladies, dude."

"I wasn't trying to impress the ladies," I mumbled in defense, trying to laugh back.

"That's good, cuz you failed pretty miserably."

I ignored him and went on my way. A little teasing on

AVAILABLE

a Monday morning was no big deal. But the teasing continued all week long. My upchucking had made bigger news than the latest football game; I was now the butt of all jokes.

"Hey, Ralph!" a girl said, nudging me as I slipped into math class. "Can't hold your liquor, huh?"

By Friday, the jokes were no longer funny. I was past the embarrassment and was now just plain angry. I'd thought these guys were my friends, but it seemed they preferred taunting over sympathizing. Why had I wasted so many weekends trying to impress these people?

A few weeks later, during health class, our teacher explained the dangers and health risks of drinking. "Alcohol is serious stuff," he told us. "Everyone's body reacts differently toward alcohol, but drinking in excess can cause all sorts of health problems; some people are actually allergic to alcohol and can't tolerate it at all."

Hmm. Allergic. Now maybe that's why I'd puked. I decided to give the story a whirl with my friends. When Friday rolled around and they began discussing the next party, I spoke up. "You know what, I'm not going to drink anymore. Because of my health, you know. I think I might be allergic to alcohol."

An acquaintance raised a skeptical eyebrow. "Really, dude? Allergic?"

"You heard our health teacher. Some people just can't tolerate it. I better lay off for a while." I hoped they'd buy my story and just leave me alone; it seemed they'd never let me live down that one fateful night.

THE PATH BACK HOME

As the weeks passed, a certain loneliness crept into my heart, and I began to feel empty inside. For years, I had filled my life with meaningless parties, booze and shallow relationships. There had to be more to life than this; there just had to!

One evening, as I cleaned out a dresser drawer I'd neglected for some time, I stumbled onto a little black Bible that I had gotten years ago. Brushing the dust off, I casually flipped through the pages. I couldn't remember the last time I'd actually read it. Suddenly, out of nowhere, a strange thought came to mind. *I wonder what Christian music sounds like?*

At the time, I honestly had no interest in Christian music whatsoever. In fact, it was the LAST thing that I was interested in! But when that fully formed thought came to my mind, it got me curious. What *does* Christian music sound like? On impulse, I wandered into the living room and thumbed through our record collection. Years before, my cousin Mike had become a Christian and had introduced his family to God. In time, several of my cousins joined a singing group called Bethesda Singers. Their church produced an album, called "The River of Life." Somehow, one of my cousins had given us a copy; I'd never listened to it before, but now seemed like as good a time as any.

As though smuggling drugs in a covert deal, I sandwiched the record between two other records and rushed back to my room.

I laughed as I inspected the guys on the cover with

AVAILABLE

their sideburns and bright burgundy suits. What was this stuff all about, anyhow?

As the upbeat music wafted through my room, I sat quietly on the bed, taking it all in. "My Lord is comin' back to this old earth again, got no time to waste in sin!" The words repeated over and over, sinking into my head. I found the tempo and the tune sort of corny, since I usually listened to heavy metal rock music, but the words struck me hard. My Sunday school teacher had often said that none of us knew how long we had left on earth, and we should not waste any time doing things that would not please God. At 8 years old, I was sure I had lots of time left on earth, so I hadn't given much thought to that message. But the emptiness in my heart the past few months had caused me to wonder if there was truly more to life than partying all weekend with my friends.

At the end of the record, a pastor gave a short but compelling message. "Turn with me real quickly to 1 John, chapter 2, verse 15," he began. "It says 'Do not love the world or the things in the world. If anyone loves the world, love for the Father is not in him. For all that is in the world, the lust of the flesh, the lust of the eyes, and the pride of life, is not of the Father but is of the world. And the world passes away, and the lust thereof, but he that does the will of God lives forever.'"

I wasn't sure if this had any bearing on my life, but I continued to listen. And then he spoke directly to me ...

"If there is anyone here tonight who is impressed by some guy who has a case of beer in the back of his car and

THE PATH BACK HOME

does a good job of squealing around corners, the Bible says that our lives are like a vapor. It's like a mist. We're here for an instant, and then it's gonna be gone. And you're gonna be 82 years old before you know it. And you'll be lying on your bed saying, 'What did I do with my life? Jesus, how could I have pushed you away from my life all of these years?' And little brothers … little sisters … I love you so much, but you're gonna be trying for the rest of your life to find what you will never find unless you turn to Jesus Christ."

I knew that what this pastor said was true. I needed to give my life over to God. Someday. Maybe I would do it later. Just as I considered this, the pastor continued to talk directly to me.

"If the Spirit of God is speaking to your heart, don't resist. Don't resist. God is not going to give you forever to turn to him. You've got this life, for man is given once to die, and then comes the judgment."

I listened with bated breath, hanging off the edge of my bed as the pastor continued to speak. I thought of my grandmother, who certainly hadn't known it was her last day on earth that afternoon as we set off for home in her little Subaru. Suddenly, I did not want to waste one more minute not knowing God.

"Hey, God, uh, it's me. Vance," I said quietly. "Uh, anyway, you know how I've messed up my life. I've really made a mess of everything. But I wanted to let you know that I'm sorry. The guy on the record was talking about having a new life, and that's what I need. So if you would

AVAILABLE

take me back, I'd like to ask you into my life again. Anyway, I guess that's it. Amen."

When I opened my eyes, I half expected to see an angel standing by the side of my bed or a bright light of some sort, but alas, my bedroom was just as it had been, a pile of dirty clothes stacked next to the door, homework papers strewn on top of my dresser. But something was different; I knew it in my heart. Something changed inside of me when I said that prayer.

Over the next couple weeks, I read through that little black Bible, poring over the words and trying to understand more about this God I had just invited into my life. Though I'd attended Vacation Bible School and sat in church many times as a child, I still had so much to learn about God. One thing was immediately clear, however: The emptiness that I'd felt the past few years was gone, replaced by something much more powerful and exciting. I had finally found a hope that mattered.

After two weeks, I finally worked up the nerve to return to the church I'd attended as a child. I approached my mother one Saturday night. "I was thinking about going back to church," I blurted. "I was planning to go tomorrow, actually."

My mother raised her brow slightly but then smiled. "Okay, if that's what you want to do, Vance, go ahead," she replied.

What will people think of me? I wondered as I trudged down the road to church the next morning. *Will they think I'm a nut like my other Christian relatives?* My heart

THE PATH BACK HOME

rate quickened and my hands grew clammy as the church building came into sight. I took a deep breath and pulled open the doors to the high school room.

Glancing around the room, I saw several of my peers from school, many whom I had partied with in weekends past. One guy sauntered up with a smirk on his face. "Who made you come to church?" he asked, rolling his eyes.

I shook my head. "No one. I came on my own." I smiled.

He looked perplexed as he walked away. Another guy walked up a few moments later. "What are you doing here, Vance?" he asked, his eyes wide.

"Just coming to check it out this morning," I replied, trying to remain confident. As I watched my former party friends mingle and laugh, I realized many of them were here this morning because their parents had forced them to come. That might have been the case for me not so long ago, but I was now here because I truly wanted a relationship with the God I'd found through a dusty old Christian record.

After the service, I approached the teacher, a man named Dale. "I really liked what you had to say today, about trusting the Lord with all our heart," I began. "I wanted to let you know that a couple weeks ago, I invited the Lord into my life. I kind of drifted away from God for a while and messed up my life. But now I'm ready to get closer with Jesus."

"That's great!" Dale said enthusiastically. "I'd be more

AVAILABLE

than happy to help you in any way I can. If you ever have any questions, I'll be here about a half hour before class. Just come in early, and we'll talk. Okay?"

"I'd love that!" I couldn't believe my ears. I had always respected Dale, but I hadn't really spoken to him since I left the church years ago. Now he was offering to give up his time to help me and to pray with me. That was far better than an invite to the best party in town.

I continued going to that little church every Sunday. I also found a Bible study for teens at the local Assembly of God church. For the next few months, I divided my time between the two churches, learning and growing as I hung out with other people who loved the Lord. The studies became the highlight of my week; I could hardly wait to get together with people who encouraged and prayed for me. I saw a genuine warmth that I hadn't experienced much of in the rest of my social circles. These folks truly cared for me, unlike my superficial acquaintances who liked me simply because I was fun to party with.

Though my father still didn't attend church or want much to do with talking about God, he respected my newfound faith. One day he came into my room and saw my Bible sitting on the floor. "Hey, son, that really doesn't belong on the ground," he said, picking it up.

"Oh, right, thanks," I replied quickly. I prayed that one day he, too, would want to have a relationship with Jesus and experience what I had.

I threw myself into football, track and band practice my senior year, studying my Bible and attending church

THE PATH BACK HOME

whenever I could. In November that year, my newfound faith was rattled to the core. Halfway through the school day, the front office called me out of my classroom. "Your mom just called. She wants you to go home right away," the lady at the desk said somberly.

"Why?" My heart jumped in my chest. "Is everything okay?"

"That's all I've learned."

Our house was just a couple blocks away, so I began walking home. Halfway home, I turned around and saw that my brother and sister were going home as well. Suddenly I knew that something was wrong. I waited for them to catch up to me.

"What's going on?" my sister asked.

"I don't know. I was just told to go home," I said, trying to stay calm.

The minute we turned the corner onto our street, I saw my dad's boss' car in the driveway. Immediately, I knew. Something terrible had happened to my dad.

My legs felt like lead as I climbed the steps to our house. My mother sat at the kitchen table with several other people. She rose to her feet, her tear-streaked face pale and anguished. "Come on in, kids," she said quietly. She then led us into a nearby bedroom.

Time seemed to stand still as we stood there quietly. Finally, Mom broke the silence. "Your dad had an accident today," she began, her voice trembling a bit. "He's dead."

Dead. My father was dead. Just like my grandmother,

AVAILABLE

he'd been snatched from our lives in the blink of an eye from a car wreck. I braced myself as the tears began to flow down my cheeks. Beside me, my brother and sister began to cry out loud. Finally my mom allowed herself to cry, her body racked with sobs over the husband she'd never see again. How could our father, a hardworking, honest man who loved his family, be gone just like that?

Grief knows no timeline or boundaries. Each of us grieved my father's loss in our own ways over the next few months. I took on many grownup responsibilities, feeling the need to hold my family together during this difficult time. To my amazement, I felt God's presence stronger than ever. On the mornings when it felt too hard to get out of bed, he comforted me with his peace, reminding me of his promise to remain near the brokenhearted. I could not imagine losing my father without the comfort from my heavenly father above.

"We're going to be okay," I told my mother one morning as I headed off to school. "You know that, right?" I smiled in an effort to cheer her up.

My mother turned from the kitchen sink and tried to smile back. "Yes, we will be okay," she replied softly. Her eyes held a certain lingering sadness these days, but I prayed that in time they would be filled with life and happiness again.

One evening, as I read my Bible, I flipped on a tape by the popular Christian band Petra. As the music wafted through the speakers, the words struck my heart. "I am available, I will come when you say go. I will stop when

THE PATH BACK HOME

you say no. My whole life was incomplete till I laid it at your feet. So use me as you will, I am available," the lead singer crooned.

And then, clear as if he was standing two feet in front of me, the Lord said to me, "Be a missionary."

I froze on my bed. Suddenly I heard it again. "Be a missionary."

Closing my Bible, I nervously asked out loud, "Lord, is that you?"

Instantly, I heard it again. "Be a missionary. Be a missionary." There was no mistake; God was clearly calling me to become a missionary. Years before, this might have baffled or frightened me, but now, as I sat in the quiet of my room, Petra singing softly in the background, an overwhelming peace came over me. I clearly knew what God wanted me to do with my life. I was to become a missionary.

I shared the exciting news with my pastor at the small Nazarene church down the street. "I really want to go on a missions trip," I told him eagerly.

"We usually take lots of missions trips, but we just don't have any coming up anytime soon," he replied. "I'll pray for you, though. I'm sure God has the perfect plan for you."

Not long after, I approached the pastor at the Assembly of God church where I attended the teen Bible study.

"You know what? I know of a church in Salem that is taking their youth group on a missions trip down to

AVAILABLE

Tijuana, Mexico, pretty soon," he said. "I'm sure I could get you on board with them."

"That would be great! By the way, what is a missionary?"

"A missionary is someone who tells people from a different culture about God. Why do you ask?"

"I just thought it was something that I should know," I replied.

I was excited. I had never gone on a missions trip in my life; I'd hardly ventured out of the small town I grew up in. It would be an adventure, but I was ready.

My cousin Kristi agreed to come on the trip with me. We set out for Los Angeles, where we spent the first week of our trip in intensive training. The night before we were to leave for Mexico, we came out to the parking lot to discover someone had slashed the tires on our bus. We patched the tires quickly, and then we were on our way. We made it halfway to the Mexican border before one of the tires exploded, and we were forced to pull off the road in the surf town of San Clemente. It was Sunday afternoon.

"I'll go phone for help," one of the youth leaders offered, hopping off the bus. He ran off to a pay phone and returned a few minutes later. "Well, unfortunately, all of the tire places seem to be closed today. Looks like we're stuck here," he said with a sigh.

We all climbed off the bus, and another youth leader gathered us to pray.

"God, we really need your help right now," he began.

THE PATH BACK HOME

"Please send someone to our assistance so that we can get back on the road and do your work."

The minute we opened our eyes, a Les Schwab tire truck drove around the corner and headed our direction. We flagged him down and explained our situation. "I was just on another call, but I'll come back in 20 minutes," he promised.

Within a couple hours, the tires on the bus were as good as new, and we were back on the road. We praised God for hearing our prayers and sending help in our time of need. The youth leaders had talked to us a great deal about spiritual warfare, explaining that Satan wanted nothing more than to thwart our plans to share the good news about God's love with others. He had certainly tried to get our bus off the road, but he hadn't succeeded.

As we neared the border, one of the youth leaders slid into the seat next to mine. "Vance, I'd really love it if you told the group about your experience with God — you know, your testimony — at one of our events down here," he said. "How do you feel about that?"

I hesitated for a moment before nodding. "Sure, I'll do it."

I was sometimes shy in new situations, but I was sure God would give me the confidence to share my story with others. After all, he had called me to be a missionary.

Tijuana was a far cry from my little town of Elgin, Oregon. My eyes grew wide as I took in the barefoot children, dusty roads and makeshift cardboard shacks. My heart began to ache for those who were physically poor,

AVAILABLE

but also for those who did not have the most valuable treasure in the world: a relationship with Christ.

One day during the trip, we stopped at a dirt soccer field and set up "camp." My pastor asked if I'd be willing to share my testimony here. As a group of teens finished a puppet skit, I gazed around at the little houses overlooking the park; a few people lingered nearby. "Now's as good a time as ever," I agreed heartily, praying that God would give me boldness.

As I spoke, a few of the guys wandered from their houses toward the field and sat down to listen. "I spent many years chasing empty things in this world. I got involved in drinking, trying to find happiness. I tried to find happiness through my friends. But none of that worked. Finally, Jesus introduced himself to me. I had turned my back on Jesus, but I discovered that he still loved me. I asked him to forgive me, and he did. But he did more than that. He gave me a new life. That is why I am here today."

As I continued to talk to the few people sitting in the field, I suddenly looked up. Overlooking the soccer field were hundreds and hundreds of apartments. To me, it looked like every window had a young man leaning out of it, listening to my story. I could tell by the look on their faces that they understood my searching heart. As I closed in prayer, scores of people streamed forward to invite the Lord into their hearts. I was thrilled and humbled that God had used me in this little dirt field in the middle of Tijuana to share the good news.

THE PATH BACK HOME

During the course of that week in Mexico, I met a pretty blond teenager named Katie. She was shy like me, but we found we had much in common; both of us had been called by God to be missionaries. "Wow, where do you think you'll end up serving?" I asked her.

"I don't know. Wherever God wants to use me," she replied lightly. Katie was from Salem and planned to attend Northwest College. I was attracted not only to her dazzling smile and pretty face but to her heart for God as well. I really hoped that our trip wouldn't be the last time I'd see her.

After returning to Oregon, Katie and I wrote letters back and forth for a few months. Each week when an envelope with her neatly printed handwriting appeared in my mailbox, a smile spread across my face. I was growing very fond of Katie and prayed about spending the rest of my life with her.

After writing to each other for quite some time, I finally moved to Katie's hometown of Salem so that I could be closer to her. That year, I asked her to marry me, and she accepted. I was thrilled to start my life together with a woman who shared my same vision. Right after our wedding, we moved to Seattle to begin our missions studies at Northwest College. Two years later, our first child, Tim, came along. Three years later, our son Steve was born, followed by another son Daniel and at last, a beautiful little girl, Joanna, to complete our family. I was thrilled that God had blessed us so abundantly, and I was ready for him to lead us in the next direction.

AVAILABLE

One day, my sister called with bad news. "Did you hear? Mom fell and broke her hip. The doctor says that it is because she has cancer. It has spread from her lungs to her bones."

"Cancer?" My heart sank. My mother had felt lost after my father's death. Our family drifted apart after she moved back to Halfway; there she sought out alcohol as a means to numb her pain. When Mom had first moved back to Halfway, my sister moved in with a Christian school teacher in order to graduate from Elgin. Eventually, Kathy accepted the Lord into her life. She was now a registered nurse in Southern Oregon and was able to care for my mother in her older age. This news came on the tail of several difficult years as Mom's health slowly declined.

"We're going to get Mom this weekend and move her in with us. I know she would love to have you come visit," my sister added.

"I'll be there," I assured her. I had asked the Lord many times about my father after his death. The Lord spoke to me, saying, "Vance, your father was as close to a Christian as he would ever be." This comforted me greatly, but after years of praying for my mother to come to Christ as well, I wondered if she'd ever have a change of heart.

It was difficult to visit my mother, even when her health was bad. Our relationship was a mess. For years, I had tried to tell her that God loved her. Yet it seemed that whenever I got closer to God, the more it divided the two of us. Mom had become an alcoholic who had little time for her family. There were times when I took my family to

THE PATH BACK HOME

visit Grandma Rose, only to have her leave to go to the bar for the evening. In fact, I had even begun to refer to her as my "birth mother," since she had no resemblance to the woman who raised me.

Over the next few months, I drove to my sister's house near Roseburg several times a week. My mom's health was declining rapidly. The lung cancer that she had contracted from years of smoking was quickly destroying her small body. Yet in the midst of that storm, we became a family once again. We began to talk and laugh and cry again in a way that we hadn't done since the death of my dad.

One day I approached my mom, who was now bedridden. "Mom, I know that we have talked about your relationship with God before. But I just wanted to ask if you would like to pray to give your life to Jesus." Mom was too weak to speak, but tears filled her eyes as she nodded her head. Kathy and I prayed with her as she accepted him into her life. My mother might not have much time left on earth, but she would now spend eternity with God in heaven. What a great comfort that was.

In September 2001, my family and I moved two hours west of Salem to become the pastor of a church in another sleepy little town, Siletz. In many ways, Siletz is just like my hometown of Elgin. It has close-knit families, hardworking people … and life-controlling addictions. The main difference is that Siletz is made up primarily of Native Americans. Little did I know that when God called me to be a missionary so many years ago, I would end up learning how to minister among such great people — on

AVAILABLE

the other side of Oregon! I love the genuine warmth of the people at Siletz Gospel Tabernacle; each person is honest about his or her struggles and eager to encourage others. God is clearly working in the hearts of the people and doing great things in our little church. I am happy to call it my home.

ಊಊಊ

"Hey, Vance, good to see you!" an old acquaintance called out with a wave.

"Hi, there!" I replied with a smile. I was back in my little hometown of Elgin. This time, though, I was leading a missions camp among a group of teenage boys in the Royal Rangers program. Just as I had gone to Tijuana to learn how to share God's love, now I was teaching the same lessons to a dozen boys from across Oregon.

It had been nearly 20 years since I'd been back. A few new stores had popped up, the paint was fading on some of the old houses and the sidewalks had a few more cracks than before, but for the most part, things hadn't changed much. As I strode along the street and passed my old church, I stopped for a moment to reflect. All that time, that church had sat there, just a few blocks from my house, an open invitation. It took me years to finally walk through those doors, but when I did, my life was never the same.

I walked past my old neighborhood, reminiscing about the many good times our family had shared in that little

THE PATH BACK HOME

doublewide trailer. In fact, I'll bet that there are still plastic army men in that garden! Our family experienced plenty of problems, but it was here in Elgin that I'd also discovered something lasting, something true: I'd found my best friend, Jesus. Coming home reminded me that sometimes it is in our own backyards that the best treasures are found.

ACCEPTED
The Story of Rayanne Moore
Written by Arlene Showalter

Apprehension

The difference of needing and being needed is a thin white line. Rayanne's lips twisted as she recalled the introduction of her book, *Thin White Line.* The heroine, Aldora, shared Rayanne's life as an artist who suffered a debilitating injury. However, unlike the author, Aldora's story ended in the saccharine-sweet lie of happily ever after.

Rayanne scratched behind Apollo's ears and sighed.

The black Great Dane cocked his head to one side, seeming to study her with his large dark eyes.

"You carry yourself like a king." Rayanne's somber mood lifted. "You certainly rule our little world, don't you, faithful friend?"

Mitzvah, a black Newfoundland mountain of canine, ambled over. "And you're the grand-daddy," Rayanne added.

Merlin, a burly Rottweiler, wedged himself between the older dogs and put his substantial paws in Rayanne's lap, preparing for the rest of him to follow.

"You big baby," she crooned. "When will you learn that you're too big to be a lap dog?"

Rayanne's hand froze on Merlin's head as a pain-filled

THE PATH BACK HOME

50-year-old memory squeezed the joy of the moment from her heart. She gathered the three massive heads close and wept.

As a young girl, Rayanne had rushed home from school on winged feet, anxious to be with her one true friend — her dog. She raced up the steps and flung open the door.

No friend met her at the door. No friend wagged a greeting. She searched every room, calling and calling for him.

"*Sei stille!* Be still," Mutter had commanded.

"*Wo ist meines Hund?*" Rayanne lifted her tear-soaked eyes. "Where's my dog?"

"I gave it away." Mother turned on her heel. "Too much bother," she tossed behind her. The cruel words skipped across the wake of her angry stride and thudded against Rayanne's stunned ears.

Breaking free of her troubled childhood memories, Rayanne clutched at her furred companions. "You will never, never leave me," she choked. "Nor I, you. I promise."

A car approached. The trio raced to the door, barking as each assumed guard position.

Rayanne's heart thudded. *Humans. Conversation. Companionship.* The ready smile dropped to a frown. *Careful.*

Humans hurt.
Humans leave.
Humans fail.

ACCEPTED

She struggled out of her seat and reached the door at the first rap, cracked it a dog's nose width and peered out. Katie and her two sons stood outside, wide smiles splitting their faces.

"Hi, Rayanne," Katie started. "We came to see if you need anything." She smiled. "Hi, Apollo, Mitzvah, Merlin. Are you guarding your mama today?"

Rayanne threw open the door. "Please come in."

The three stepped inside. "Rayanne," Katie cried, "it's freezing in here!"

Rayanne nodded. "I cannot generate enough energy to bring in wood for the stove."

"Tim, Steven," Katie ordered, "go split some firewood for Rayanne, and bring it into the house."

The boys loped to the backyard and tackled the chore.

"Sit down, Rayanne," Katie continued, "while I make us a nice cup of tea."

Rayanne sank down into her favorite chair. The dogs encircled her at once. "Sounds exquisite," she agreed.

The ladies chatted as the boys chopped.

"I didn't think Oreo would let us in." Katie grinned, referring to Rayanne's horse. "He checked us out thoroughly before allowing any of us to open the car doors."

Harley, the indomitable cat, hopped up into Rayanne's lap, turned three times and then settled in for a grooming session.

Rayanne passed a hand over his back. A tear worked its way from one eye and trickled down her worn cheek.

THE PATH BACK HOME

"I love them all so much," she said. "They've never let me down."

Katie waited.

"My parents were so *schwer* — excuse me, difficult," Rayanne said, slipping back to the German of her childhood. "So strict, cold, unloving." She stopped, circling her cup with a teaspoon.

"When I was a teen …" Rayanne paused to gaze out the window, past her lush Oregon pastureland, past the distant California border — all the way to Los Angeles and 40 years back, "I learned they weren't my parents at all." The teaspoon circled the cup again.

"My father, Raymond Moore, died during military maneuvers in California before I was born." She stroked Harley.

"My mother died of cancer soon after. I never knew them." She busied her hands with the teaspoon.

"How did you learn?" Katie's voice floated, soft and encouraging.

Rayanne's lips locked. *Watch out, Rayanne,* she admonished herself. *Trust only four-legged furry creatures. Not humans.*

Silence stretched taut between the women. Rayanne stared at nothing. Katie smiled.

"I discovered the truth as a teen," Rayanne explained at length, "by accident. I felt so hurt. It seemed the whole world was in on the lie except me. As soon as I could do so legally, I dropped my grandparents' last name, Gierlich, and took my dad's."

ACCEPTED

The back door slapped open. Tim and Steven hauled in armloads of split easy-to-handle-sized wood and stacked each piece neatly near the wood-burning stove. Tim stoked life into the fire and added fresh wood. Rayanne waited until the boys returned to the woodpile outside.

"I attempted to locate my dad's family, but never could," she continued. "I felt like I had been robbed of identity." She drew a deep breath. "Who was I? It haunted me all my life. My parents — *grandparents* — isolated themselves and me from life. I was so alone."

Katie rose on silent feet, refilled the teacups and sat again.

"I left for college and never looked back. I tried marriage …" Rayanne paused again, raising a shaky cup to her lips. "We were both musicians. He played a wonderful guitar. But, he left me, just like my parents. People hurt, abandon, fail …"

The dogs, sensing her pain, moved close. Rayanne's hands stayed busy, patting first one head, then another, interspersed with sips of tea.

"I took a job as a lineman for the telephone company," Rayanne continued. "Back when women were expected to stay at home and raise children. Every man refused to work with me." Rayanne's one hand reached behind her, rubbing her back.

"One day, I was working alone in a manhole without assistance — no lookout. Someone threw something into the hole. Instinctively I jumped back. A piece of rebar — that reinforces cement — stuck in my back."

THE PATH BACK HOME

The boys returned with their next load, stacked and left.

"Now, I was not only alone, but injured, disabled. I began writing — writing what I wished life would be, rather than what it was." Rayanne's mouth twisted. "Harlequin published my first novel in '83, *Thin White Line*. I was just thinking about that book before you arrived. 'The difference of needing and being needed is a thin white line,'" she quoted. "That's the intro."

"What was the book about?" Katie asked.

Rayanne laughed a harsh, unhappy puff. "Me, but with a different ending. My heroine, Aldora, suffered a severe spinal injury, but surgery enabled her to return to her passion of painting murals. I wrote an ending I never lived — that of the proverbial Prince Charming riding in and extending passionate and everlasting love. That's where our two lives part ways." Rayanne barked another laugh.

"Writing, painting, composing all brought a beauty into my life," Rayanne mused. "Beauty that I never experienced in reality. I wrote romances, spinning stories of what I wished could be for my life."

Merlin tried to nose Harley from Rayanne's lap so he could fill it. Harley swiped at him with a no-nonsense paw, and Merlin retreated. Rayanne smiled at the exchange.

"I went from writing happily-ever-after stories to writing ones of revenge. I met another author, and we worked together on a screenplay. Our heroine was murdered by her husband, but after reincarnation, set out to murder him." Rayanne shook her head. "My soul

ACCEPTED

descended into the ebony darkness of distrust. I swore off humans forever."

A small smile softened her mouth. "But we also wrote a series of fun who-done-its. Again, our heroine was similar to me; middle-aged, alone and independent. Fanny Zindel solved mysteries everywhere she went," Rayanne added.

"But, stories are just that — stories. I could craft events any way I desired them to go. But I still felt empty — longing for something, someone." She sighed.

"How did you come to God?" Katie asked.

Rayanne's face brightened at once. "Pastor James. God bless him!"

Katie nodded and smiled. Pastor James Van Etten had served as the pastor of the Logsden Neighborhood Church for several years and was well-known for his infectious smile and his love for kids.

"I loved to walk. The pain was there regardless, so I walked. I used two sticks to aid me.

"One night I was walking along Old River Road when a van stopped." She paused.

"I believe it was almost 11. I remember it was quite late. The driver leaned across the seat and asked if I wanted a lift. 'No, thank you,' I said. 'I'm fine.' He turned out to be Pastor James. He and his daughter were driving home from a nearby Bible study.

"He asked me about my walking sticks and why I needed them. I explained that I experienced frequent muscle spasms in my legs and back." Merlin edged to her

THE PATH BACK HOME

chair, keeping a wary eye on Harley. Her fingers ruffled his ears.

"He asked if he could pray for me. You can imagine my shock! Why would a stranger want to pray for a stranger? I shrugged and said okay. What could it hurt?"

Apollo appeared to nod in solemn agreement. Mitzvah rested a slobbery chin on her knee.

"He prayed for me and then invited me to the Bible study. 'It's held at the Schones' house right over there.' He pointed. I said I would come." She paused again.

"I waited a few weeks. Why should I trust these people? Everybody embraces for a while before pushing away. But I finally started going. One night, after the Bible study, Pastor James asked if the group could pray for my healing. Again I thought, *What's the harm of it?*

"They gathered around me and prayed. I felt nothing." She shrugged. "But then, I expected nothing. I stood up when it came time to leave. 'Oh, wow,' I said. 'I don't feel any pain!' I took a few steps. 'No pain!' I said. The whole group started clapping and saying things like, 'Praise you, Jesus.'" She touched each knee. "I still marvel at that.

"Then Roberta Schones invited me to come to another meeting, a prayer meeting, held in her home one morning a week." Rayanne stopped to search her memory.

"I think it was on Tuesdays. After the meeting, Pastor James asked if I would like to accept the Lord into my life."

Rayanne nodded as the boys returned from another wood-gathering trip.

ACCEPTED

"Sit down and warm yourselves," she invited.

"I had embraced the spiritual introspection of New Age and Buddhism, but neither filled the colossal longings that haunted me. So, why not try Jesus? I agreed, and we all prayed together. Immediately, I felt different — complete, accepted." She wiped a tear from one eye.

"I came to trust God right away," she said. "However, people — that was a different matter. People had always let me down, left me, hurt me."

I'm still not 100 percent sure why you and other Christians keep coming around.

Katie smiled. Rayanne surveyed the animal guard about her.

"I'd smile and let them in, but my heart still questioned, *Why are they here, what do they want and when are they going to abandon me?*" Rayanne lifted her shoulders.

"When I attended the Logsden church, I guess I was still very wary. I was looking for a reason to leave before I could be hurt. And so I did. That's when I started attending Siletz Gospel Tabernacle. I thought I would only stay for a little while ... but God started to change my heart. I have finally begun to see God's love through other people ... through all of you."

"I'm glad you're starting to accept us," Katie said. "It seems after having that stroke, you could use some regular assistance. The Lord put you on my heart, so here we are," she added.

"How about our agreeing to come two times a week to

THE PATH BACK HOME

check on you? That way, you're assured of plenty of wood for a warm house."

Rayanne nodded. "That sounds wonderful."

Anticipation

She looked forward to those bi-weekly visits more than she cared to admit. *But, how long will it last?* she wondered. *It's just a matter of time before the church abandons me, I'm sure.*

The visits continued, week after week, year after year, until July 26, 2005 approached.

"How about a party?" Katie asked. "For your 60th birthday?"

Tears bathed Rayanne's eyes. "I've never had a birthday party," she choked.

"Never?" Katie asked, shocked.

"Not once," Rayanne insisted.

"Then it's about time," Katie declared, with an emphatic shake of her head.

Approval

"This is *your* party," Katie exclaimed. "You're the guest of honor. You're not supposed to bring anything!"

"I brought a poem — for Jesus," Rayanne explained. "A tribute to his protection over me."

"Please read it," Katie encouraged.

ACCEPTED

Lord, I know you can set your hedge around
No one knows that better than I — how profound
For I felt Satan lash out and knock me to my knees
I felt your wings enfold me, I even felt their breeze

Rayanne's eyes filled. "God has shown me total love — complete acceptance. He took me just as I was, bitter, confused, starved and lonely, and brought me into his bosom. I took care of myself for years because I thought nobody cared about me. Then God brought all of you into my life to show me that not only did *he* care, but others cared as well.

"I was totally self-sufficient all those years. Then I learned that God was waiting for me at the end of my independence."

Rayanne threw out her arms as if to embrace the whole group.

"I love God. And I love you. Thank you. Thank you for this lovely party. You all are my real family."

"Therefore, if anyone is in Christ, he is a new creation;
the old has gone, the new has come!"
(2 Corinthians 5:17).

THE PATH BACK HOME

<u>The Bargain</u>
By Rayanne Moore

Oh Lord, what do I do?
There's a question in my heart
I want to give myself to you
But don't know how to start

Then came His voice from up above
Just take my hand, my dearest child
Step out on the void, said Love
With a voice so meek and mild

Step out upon the emptiness
With faith and with belief
Step out into the void and find
The rock that lies beneath

So I took one trembling step
And gripped my Savior's hand
I stepped out into yawning space
At His express command

Now I won't say that ever since
Life's been just joy and more
I won't say that sorrows
Did not line up at my door

When one it curled upon the mat
The other walked right in
From sorrow, painful dark and deep
There Satan offered sin

ACCEPTED

But I will tell you since that day
He for me came alive
As each woe had its sport with me
He helped me to survive

And since I trusted Him I found
My Savior's always there
Though I was mired within my loss
He kept me from despair

I won't tell you each day began
Without attending grief
But Jesus ever faithful true
Gave strength and sweet relief

Well I won't say my road has been
Free of the slippery slope
But I will say I trusted Him
And He restored my hope

I will not say that life has been
Without its shifting sand
When Satan struck me down with pain
My Savior helped me stand

I will not say He made life clear
And all my questions ceased
But He gave strength unto each day
And health and joy increased

THE PATH BACK HOME

And never will I loose my hold
Upon my Savior's hand
When I step out into that void
I find His solid land

I still won't say life's been ideal
Since I gave faith a start
But my Savior gave His hand to me
And I gave Him my heart

CONCLUSION

You have just read seven different stories of hope, and I trust that they have been an encouragement to you. Yet there are many more stories like these. In fact, the Bible itself tells a wonderful story of hope in the book of Luke. This story is often called the "Prodigal Son."

It tells of a young man who desperately wanted to experience the "wild side" of life. One day he approached his father and told him that he couldn't wait until his father was dead. He wanted his inheritance, and he wanted it NOW!

Surprisingly, the father granted his son's bizarre request and gave him his share of the estate. So with eyes set on worldly adventure and his pockets full of money, the son ran away from his father's home and headed off to the bright lights of the big city.

For a brief time, life was full of pleasure and freedom. Yet as time went on, his pleasure-centered lifestyle slowly began to lose its attractiveness. Rather than being a path to freedom, he found that his extravagant life was actually leading him down a path toward bondage and slavery. Eventually his money ran out … and so did his hope. His wild living, which started out so easily, had cost him more than he had ever expected. His life was destroyed, his future was destroyed and he found himself penniless and friendless.

THE PATH BACK HOME

Out of desperation, he found a miserable job that would at least pay a few of his bills: He became a pig farmer. One morning he got up early to feed the pigs. As he looked down at the pig food, he became hungry and wished that he could eat the pig slop himself. In that moment, he suddenly saw things clearly. He came to the startling realization of how low his life had taken him. He had truly hit rock bottom. The son thought to himself, *Why should I be here in a pigpen when my own father's servants are treated so much better than this?* It was at that moment that the boy made a brave decision. He would return home and beg his father to take him back as a hired worker.

With great courage, the prodigal son got up and left the filth of the pigpen to begin the long walk back home. As he walked back toward the home that he had run away from, one question kept coming to his mind. *How would his father treat him?* He knew that he was undeserving of anything from his father. He had just done too many bad things ...

Walking mile after mile down the road, the son began to rehearse what he would say to his father when he saw him next. "Father, I have sinned against heaven and against you. I no longer deserve to be your son. Please make me like one of your hired servants." He expected the worst — but his father was truly the only hope he had. And so he kept walking down the path that led back home.

At the other end of that long road, the father was again gazing out at the gate that led toward the farm. Since his

CONCLUSION

son had left home so long ago, he spent much of his day looking out at this gate. *Where was his son today? Was he okay? Was he even alive?* Once again, his troubled thoughts led him to pray for the day when his wayward child would finally return home. As the father struggled to control his troubled thoughts, he turned again to look down the distant road ... and noticed something different.

Looking closer, he saw a homeless beggar coming his way. The beggar was covered in filthy rags, and his long greasy hair covered his face as he slowly stumbled down the dirt path. But there was something different about this beggar. It was the way that he walked. He had seen that walk before ...

His mind began to flash back to an earlier time. And then he remembered it. The moment when his own little boy let go of his finger for the first time and took his very first steps across the living room. Joy came upon the father's face as he suddenly realized something startling: That homeless beggar was his own long-lost son! Disregarding all sense of "proper" actions, the father suddenly burst through the door and ran out of the house. He sprinted down the long, dusty road toward the boy. Toward *his* boy!

As the son looked out toward the house that he had left so long ago, he saw some movement. Looking closer, he realized that his father was running toward him. The son became even more nervous. Never before had he seen his father run like this! Was his father *that* mad at him? Doubts began to flood the boy's mind. What was he doing

THE PATH BACK HOME

here? Why had he come? This was a mistake. But it was too late. And he had nowhere else to turn. The son had carefully practiced what he would say to his father ... and now it was time. So, with a shaky voice, he began his prepared speech as soon as the father was close enough to hear him.

"Father, I have sinned against heaven and against you ..."

But the father wasn't listening. And he didn't stop running until he got to the boy. With great joy he threw his arms around the stinky, homeless beggar and began to kiss his dirty face again and again and again. "Quick," the father finally yelled to his servants, "get a robe for him to wear and get sandals for his feet. Get my family ring for him to wear on his finger, and kill the fattened calf. We're going to have a great celebration, because this son of mine was dead, and he is alive again. He was lost, but now he is found."

And the party of a lifetime began.

It may sound too good to be true, but that is how God welcomes *every* wayward child back home. When Jesus told this story, it was because a number of people were criticizing him for spending too much time with "sinners." Jesus responded by telling them that they were *absolutely* right! Jesus loves sinners. And God the Father loves sinners. More than that, he lives for the moment when just one of his broken, filthy children humbly comes back home to begin life over again. *That* is the heart of God. A God of second chances!

CONCLUSION

We are all in need of a new relationship with God. No one needs religion. No one needs another place to go and be judged. We all need the love and acceptance and hope that comes from giving our lives over to God and learning how to live a life filled with hope.

The people that you read about in this book meet together most Sunday mornings in Siletz at the corner of Logsden Road and Palmer Street. Yes, it's a church building, but the people inside will welcome you into their hearts and lives. They will help you find God and grow closer to him. They want to be there when God meets you on the path to welcome you back home.

Back to a home where you belong!

So, if you would like, we invite you to come on by and check it out. More than anything else, though, take some time right now to talk to God. Just talk to him. He's right there where you are, and he loves you very much. If you would like more information and you have Internet access, check us out at www.SiletzGT.com.

We look forward to walking with you on the road back home!

We would love for you to join us!

We meet Sunday mornings at 11 a.m. at
164 NE Palmer Street, Siletz, OR 97380.

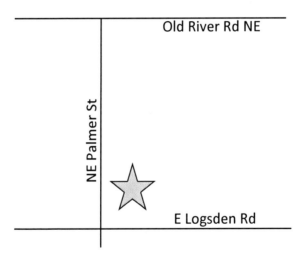

Please call us at 541.444.2564 for directions, or
contact us at www.siletzgt.com.

For more information on reaching your city with stories from your church, please contact Good Catch Publishing at www.goodcatchpublishing.com

GOOD CATCH PUBLISHING

Did one of these stories touch you? Did one of these real people move you to tears? Tell us (and them) about it on our reader blog at www.goodcatchpublishing.blogspot.com.